Lev DODIN

JOURNEY WITHOUT END

Reflections and Memoirs
PLATONOV Observed:
Rehearsal Notes

Foreword by Peter Brook

*With translation from the Russian
by Oksana Mamyrin
and Anna Karabinska*

Edited by John Ormrod

Tantalus Books

First published in Great Britain 2005
by Tantalus Books Limited
11 Hollycroft Avenue London NW3 7QG

Reflections and Memoirs copyright © Lev Dodin, 2004
Platonov Observed: Rehearsal Notes © Lev Dodin, Anna Ogibina
Translation from the Russian copyright © Anna Karabinska,
Oksana Mamyrin
This collection copyright © Tantalus Books Limited, 2004

The authors have asserted their moral rights.

British Library Cataloguing-in-Publication Data
A CIP catalogue record for this book is available
from the British Library

Tantalus Books Limited Reg. No. 4200857

ISBN 0 9542944 2 4

Book Design Nadezhda Oleg Lyahova
Typeset by IDA Advertising Agency
Printed by Expressprint Ltd, Sofia

Acknowledgements

*We would like to express
our gratitude to Svetlana Druzhinina,
who helped with the selection and editing of the
Russian text of REFLECTIONS AND MEMOIRS
and to Maria Semikina who contributed
to the translation.
Our thanks go to Vladimir Kantor
and Elena Alexandrova from the press department
of the Maly Drama Theatre
who provided the photographs for the illustrations
and to Maria Ganeva for her invaluable
help and support.*

Contents

Foreword
Beyond Theatre

Directing is a terrible word. It covers the best and the worst in theatre. There are directors who abuse their power, there are one-sided directors, whose direction is mainly visual or textual, acrobatic or psychological. Lev Dodin is one of the rare exceptions who has it all. His work shows his mastery of the multiple skills theatre demands, from running a company to preparing an ensemble, from creating a space to inhabiting the space, filling it with the rich material that he has cultivated with his actors and helped to grow. This book is a living record of what Dodin has discovered on the spot, in simple practical terms. Excellently captured in English, you feel you can hear his voice, undogmatic, unpretentious - speaking to you as to his actors - with intimacy and warmth. He reveals how he probes, listens, searches and brings to his task the pain and conflicts of his own life. And even when he says disarmingly he is not interested in comedy, his compassionate laughter is never far away.

Lev was formed in a tough school, the Soviet system, to which he never yielded. From Stanislavsky, Meyerhold and the other great pioneers of directing he took what was best without becoming prisoner of any method or doctrine. In his work the imagination flows freely and the forms change as they reflect a search for the details of human truth.

In his production of "Brothers and Sisters", the joy at first was theatrical. It came from knowing we were in a theatre, watching a flawless ensemble, unfolding a fascinating story. Then came the unexpected. Suddenly, one of the fictional characters opened a paper parcel and placed on the table a loaf of bread. This was real, it was the thing itself, the story gave it a poignant meaning. The coup de theatre shattered theatre. The characters and the audience lived the same experience. Something had penetrated beyond artistry. For me, the whole of Lev is in that moment, as an artist, as a man in life and as a friend.

PETER BROOK

Lev Dodin, Peter Brook, Tatyana Shestakova and Natasha Parry with St. Petersburg Mayor Anatoliy Sobchak, 1993.
Photographer Victor Vasilyev

Lev Dodin, Peter Brook, Natasha Parry, Dusseldorf, Germany, 1992.
Photographer Victor Vasilyev

Lev Dodin and Giorgio Strehler.
Archive of the Maly Drama (MDT)

Lev Dodin,
Alexey Poray-Koshits,
Joseph Brodsky during
the tour of *Gaudeamus*,
New York, 1994.
Archive MDT

Lev Dodin and Eduard Kochergin
at the rehearsal
of *The Possessed*,
Braunschweig, Germany, 1991.
Photographer Yuri Belinsky

Lev Dodin, Mstislav Rostropovich and Mikhail Baryshnikov during the tour of *Brothers and Sisters*, Japan, 1989. Photographer Yuri Belinsky.

Lev Dodin, Natalya Akimova
and Oleg Borisov rehearsing
A Gentle Creature, Bolshoy Drama
Theatre, St. Petersburg, 1981.
Archive MDT

Lev Dodin and Innokenti Smoktunovsky
rehearsing *The Golovlev Family*, Moscow
Arts Theatre, 1984. Archive of MDT.

Lev Dodin at the rehearsal of *Chevengur*, 1999.
Photographer Victor Vasilyev

Reflections and Memoirs

Lev Dodin, in the 1970's.
Archive MDT

Lev Dodin and Tatyana Shestakova
rehearsing *The Cherry Orchard* in
the village of Molodezhnoe, 1993.
Photographer Victor Vasilyev

THE EVOLUTION OF AN UNFETTERED QUEST

Why did you choose to work in the theatre? When you were young did you like acting, pretending to be somebody else or imagining other worlds?

Like all children I loved to act: not just to put on a mask but to conjure up another life. Perhaps this was born out of our monotonous daily existence, but acting opened up amazing horizons for me. For instance, while walking along a Soviet street wearing my pioneer's tie, I could imagine myself as a marquis hurrying to meet the king. This is a very human desire - to long for another existence, another destiny and it is just the manifestation of a hidden desire for immortality.

One could say that it is the dream of immortality that brings people to the theatre - subconsciously they want to live out different lives and theatre gives them this opportunity. It becomes obvious in an instant, in a school theatre or a drama club where today you act the villain, tomorrow you can become a hero and the day after that an old woman. Your experiments may not be a professional performance, but you have breathed the air of freedom. And on top of that, once you've taken control over your own and other potential lives, you start to imagine yourself as (dare I say it) Demiurge the Creator. This is the greatest possible pleasure a person can savour.

However, it is only today that I can rationalise it. In those days I just allowed myself to be swept along. I was lucky, after the frolics of my childhood, to get into the remarkable Young Viewer's Theatre (YVT), where Matvey Grigorievich Dubrovin, a pupil of the great Vsevolod Meyerhold, was director. He was a lonely man with a difficult personal life and, unlike us youngsters, had a profound understanding of the system which governed our daily lives. He did not have any close friends to talk to, so he talked to us. I discovered that in Theatre it was possible to talk about everything. Theatre became the main priority in my life, the place where everything could be discussed seriously and openly, just as it was never possible in everyday life. It lifted us above the routine and at the same time gave us a chance to learn about the world around us. Although we never discussed politics with Matvey Grigorievich, we nonetheless understo-

od that our lives were different from the lives of ordinary people.

Matvey Grigorievich was also an incredibly talented director. I remember his rehearsals even now, the remarkable sense of rhythm which appeared in the scenes he directed. It was as if suddenly a metronome started beating, not literally but internally. Whatever previously had lacked rhythm would suddenly acquire an inner pulse. Matvey Grigorievich was physically unprepossessing - a short, balding Jew with big eyes and a large forehead - but when he started to perform everything he did was fantastic. He took on dozens of personalities, and immediately the theatre came alive. Something fragmentary, incomprehensible and without merit (most of the time we were rehearsing second rate Soviet plays) became transformed into an intoxicating performance. It didn't last long because none of us could replicate it. But I remember very well this possibility of raising the commonplace to extraordinary heights, and conjuring up drama out of a void.

These were the first lessons I received about my profession. It was then that Theatre became a little corner of freedom in our (as I can see now) circumscribed lives. It was not obvious to us then, but we became addicted to YVT, and spent all day there. We would leave around midnight and could hardly say goodbye; standing for hours at the corner talking and talking. We loved being together. This sensation - delight in each other's company - is forever connected in my mind with Theatre.

Very early on we appreciated the contrast between the inner strength of this man and his social status. Managers despised him, his colleagues patted him condescendingly on the shoulder. We became aware of the absurdity of this situation, and sensed the latent power in the person who can create and the independence of someone who seemed superficially to be dependent. This taught me an important lesson for the rest of my life. Theatre became a way of life, expecting you to be independent and endowing you with this independence.

It's surprising to hear that your first teacher was a pupil of Meyerhold. You were always thought to be a direct pupil of Stanislavsky,

but it looks as if you inherited the idea of the ensemble company, of the company of like-minded people from the YVT.

One of my teachers was directly connected with Stanislavsky and another with Meyerhold. So probably I absorbed from the milk of my theatre-parents this idea that theatre is not only an important part of life, but life itself.

The discovery belongs to Stanislavsky who, together with Nemirovich-Danchenko, built the Moscow Arts Theatre at the end of the 19th century using the example of the Russian Imperial Theatres as well as that of the German theatres belonging to Count Mannheim. Stanislavsky and Nemirovich-Danchenko were the first to put theatre on a par with great literature. It is well known that great literature exists in time. It is written in a certain time, but nevertheless changes with time. You can go back to this literature and discover something new. The same can happen to a theatre production.

This example of the Moscow Arts Theatre has since inspired people to create ensembles, to create a theatre governed by the spirit. For example, there was the Sovremennik which was founded in the fifties, and then the Taganka Theatre also in Moscow led by Yuri Lyubimov. This was very important, particularly for Russia, because after 1917 religion attracted persecution and was ousted from the consciousness of the people. Even before the revolution, the official religion, the religion of the state, didn't satisfy artists; that religion was too close to the ruling classes and was bound by dogma. That is why the idea of the arts as a kind of religious cult was always strong in Russia.

Stanislavsky was a genius. He saw the theatre as a specific artistic space that has to be created, that has to be lived in under its own laws; a space where you exist not only with your body, but most of all with your soul. You may not like Stanislavsky's thoughts but they are like Newton's laws, they are totally objective. If the actor plays in the right way he plays in Stanislavsky's way even if he doesn't like it – that's the paradox. Stanislavsky has found the formula of theatre, of serious theatre, although some of his methods have become dated. The essence of his discovery is that theatre is a constant search for the ideal, a constant striving for perfection. Thus practice and trai-

ning are everything. He was changing the means all the time but the essence remained everlasting and true. It is difficult to attain it and even more difficult to live by it. There isn't a single theatre today where actors train and practice every day and it's not because they don't believe in Stanislavsky, it's because they are lazy.

The idea of the ensemble theatre really first came to me from my teacher Matvey Grigorievich Dubrovin who was a pupil of Meyerhold. But this only shows how relative everything is. Meyerhold himself was a pupil of Stanislavsky.

I was fortunate for the second time at the Theatre Academy in meeting Boris Vulfovich Zon - a remarkably gifted man and a different type of teacher. Zon was a very professional person, dapper and somewhat closed and reserved. After the war during the Stalin years, his pupils denounced him demanding his dismissal as an anti-Soviet person. He was forced to leave the academy and spent a few years without a job. I met him after he was given back his teaching post. Stalin had died by then and the period of the thaw had begun. The title of "Professor" suited him very much in that old-fashioned sense which now is almost unknown. Every year he had a new suit made by a good tailor, and renewed his collection of bow ties. I remember so well his first lecture to us, his first year students. He arrived in a snow-white suit, which was extremely rare at that time. Then he took off his jacket, showing off a superb white shirt underneath, and threw it on a rickety chair in the lecture hall. What a showman!

He spoke little about life as such. The material he had chosen for his teaching had nothing to do with reality, because for him it was easier to talk about abstract matters. But he was professional to the core, and every gesture was very important to him. Unfortunately today, for different reasons, professionalism of this calibre is vanishing, if it has not disappeared already. At the end of the 1930's Zon worked in the Leningrad Young Viewer's Theatre as director and teacher, supervising an undergraduate group of very talented students, which managed to produce some remarkable performances. That was the beginning of a new YVT and Zon became its director and a very popular man in the city. Handsome and charming, he enjoyed success with women and wasn't ashamed of it.

On one occasion he told us a rather revealing story. In 1917, while he and his fellow students were rehearsing a play in a big hall at somebody's house, they were disturbed by a fracas from the street. So they closed the windows, then the curtains and finally the shutters. The noise was still audible but they managed to concentrate and finish their rehearsal. The following day they were surprised to learn that the previous day the Kremlin had been attacked (no less), cannons fired and the Soviets had taken over power. He told us this story when I was in my final year, and I thought then that I would have been ashamed to admit to being engaged in rehearsals at the outset of the Revolution. Only later did I understand that one of the very few people who were, on that day in 1917, engaged in something worthwhile was my teacher.

At a time when he was already well known, one day he read a copy of an as yet unpublished book by Stanislavsky "An Actor Prepares". He was so impressed with it, and all his conceptions about theatre changed so dramatically that he went to Moscow. There he managed to get in touch with Stanislavsky and, for years until his death, every Thursday he would take the train to Moscow and go to classes on Leontievsky Pereulok where the great K.S. lived. Then on Sunday nights he would return to Leningrad to manage the theatre and direct performances.

Zon's love for Stanislavsky was contagious. He used to tell us a funny story that when Stanislavsky's book came out with all his thoughts about how he had failed in this role and hadn't succeeded in that one, an actor exclaimed: "There you are! KS was a lousy actor". "I saw all these roles", Zon would tell us "and he was brilliant. Brilliant - but always dissatisfied". In fact, in his old age he would lock himself in a cupboard and start doing his voice exercises. Only a great and amazing madman would do that. How tragic are his notes on the making of Bulgakov's *Moliere*. It was thought to be a failure, they would say, because Stanislavsky didn't understand Bulgakov. But he worked and worked on it, turning every corner of the plot into a search for perfection, and I am convinced that, had he had enough time, he would have found Bulgakov's *Moliere*. Isn't that what we all do in the theatre – pay our dues to this delight in the unknown and impossible?

When we students used to offer him what we thought was a bold solution for a scene, he would reply: "You want me to repeat the mistakes of my youth. I have already been a formalist". And we thought then "you old…". We didn't use the word "fool", but we meant it. Only later did I realise that he really had already been a formalist, and that our neophyte revelations were nothing new to him, but a repetition of his past, re-inventing the wheel so to speak, ideas which sometimes even nowadays impress the imagination of novices.

There is still very little written about Stanislavsky's last years - the years when he re-invented his system. From the rather strict method which many considered his system to be, he came to believe in the "logic or evolution of the unfettered quest", the quest into the boundless life of the free human spirit, which is difficult to describe and even more difficult to grasp. Actually, at home on Leontievsky Pereulok he was busy searching for these instants of "living experience", which could sometimes miraculously occur at rehearsal.

When Zon used to recollect Konstantin Sergeevich (KS as he called him from sheer force of his old studio habit), he would make a gesture pointing to the sky. We thought he was speaking about Stanislavsky as a God, but later it turned out that he had lectured for ten years in a hall with a portrait of Stanislavsky hung above him. He moved to another lecture hall but the gesture remained. Here is the nature of a gesture, the origin of an image. But I still think this explanation a simplistic one, although it is partly true. Nonetheless Stanislavsky was a godlike being.

What do you think was the main thing your teacher inherited from Stanislavsky?

When I saw the first documentary about Stanislavsky in the 70's, I suddenly felt that I had already known this man – the familiar gestures, the way he lifted his head - and I realised that I had seen Boris Vulfovich doing the same things. He didn't copy Stanislavsky; it became part of his own nature. But in my opinion the main thing he inherited was the trust in another human being, in human nature, in strong individuality. He adored individuality.

I often overheard him talking to other lecturers. He would tell colleagues: "Do not teach the student to speak well. Let her speak the way she does naturally. You might want to teach her to speak like everybody else, but she should speak her own way". Sometimes it was overdone - a student needs some discipline. But Zon adored personality, and that was at the time when little importance was given to personality. In Russian theatre the ability to transform, to impersonate has always been very important. For Zon the most interesting thing was how human individuality, human nature survives and develops. He trusted actors enormously. And his own role, that of director, became for him absolutely secondary, subservient. He assumed that a director could only help an actor, but that an actor originates everything himself.

That's my theatrical genealogy, and it's easier to talk about it than about myself. I think what I am doing now, perhaps, would have seemed strange to both my teachers because tastes change with the passage of time. But all the time I believe I keep doing what I used to do at their classes. Maybe combining these two almost opposite characters might be the most interesting thing that I do.

It is understandable why you decided to create your own theatre – it is in the spirit of the tradition. But how did it all start?

To some extent I am following the tradition which I received from both my teachers and the books I read. The cult of Stanislavsky was absolute then. This cult was very Soviet, very unyielding. But on the other hand I think that young people need a legend. It provides support and makes them push themselves. Stanislavsky's legend fascinated us - the legend of an intelligent, human theatre and not a discreditable one. And I must say you come across discreditable productions quite often. We saw large numbers of them when we were young. Then there are the stories and gossip of the theatre academy. Boris Vulfovich used to say: "These walls are saturated with the stench of banality - this is the most anti-artistic place in the world". Whatever we saw around us, with very few exceptions, contradicted what we read in our favourite books.

And so from our childhood sensations, from books and from our ir-

ritation with banality, a perception of theatre as a rescue from the commonplace was born. It is a very egotistical thing, by the way. I generally think that theatre is fundamentally egotistical because on the whole nothing preoccupies the human heart quite so much as thinking about ourselves, our own worries and emotional experiences. Nothing absorbs us as much as sorting out our own life's problems. If you spend time thinking about these problems of yours, these concerns can be very helpful to others. Perhaps one of the tragedies of our country is this lack of interest in ourselves.

So this egotistical concern, I believe, served as a spur for the creation of our theatre, of our company. Additionally there was the joy of communicating with students, because with students it was possible to talk about anything you wanted in any way you wanted. The company made it possible to offer them "conditions of work" which I thought made sense. When in 1983 I was offered the position of artistic director of the Maly Theatre, I began my work by inviting my former students to this very little – because Maly means 'little' in Russian – theatre, which was in all respects (and still is) a very modest building housed within a block of flats.

However for a long time you worked as a visiting director.
The years before the Maly were awful and wonderful, both at the same time. When you work as a visiting director in different theatre companies there is no formal responsibility. You are absolutely free and the only thing you are risking is your reputation, since they might never invite you to direct a performance in their theatre or anywhere else again.

You could take risks or you could avoid them, but in either event there was no formal responsibility. You did not have to be in charge and could still do whatever you wanted. As a general rule freedom is a great thing, a great opportunity. As a matter of fact, for ten years I enjoyed it, although now I can't understand how my wife and I lived: I was earning next to nothing and moreover was not earning regularly.

But it was a happy time. With just responsibilities for directing, it was possible to establish exceptional relationships with the actors,

similar to those with my pupils. Interestingly, quite often I was warned about somebody's bad temper while in reality they were nice people. I had the chance to work with great actors and it was an amazing experience. I found it easier to work with them, especially if you can offer them something "allowing room for growth". This is very important in theatre - to come across a task which makes you feel your own shortcomings. In overcoming these shortcomings you learn about yourself and about life.

It is the dream of mediocrity to avoid problems at any cost. Talented people are different, because talent is like a mould which consumes them and makes them doubt, makes them feel dissatisfied and long for something else. A thousand questions from Innokenti Smoktunovsky could have driven me mad if I had not had my own two thousand questions for him in return. This mutual questioning made us allies and we even developed a friendly relationship at work, because we both realised that we had room for growth.

The same situation applied with Oleg Borisov. When we started to work on Dostoevsky's *A Gentle Creature*, the first thing he said was: "I don't know how to act." I remember his very words "Could I be your pupil?" and I had the effrontery to say OK, because it seemed natural to me. Obviously he was not a pupil but a powerful collaborator, but his attention and poignancy were like those of a talented pupil, every teacher's dream which very rarely comes true.

In spite of that you accepted the offer to become a director of the Maly Drama Theatre.

At first I was …scared. I did not want to be a manager. Partly because when I had directed in other theatres, I realised very well what it meant to be the principal director. I had been connected with The Maly Drama Theatre previously since I used to bring my pupils there one after another. I had directed quite a few plays there and some of them were close to my heart, especially Abramov's *The House*. But I turned down the offer. Nevertheless they kept ringing me and I kept hesitating.

It was all decided, however awful it may sound, by Fyodor Abramov's death. He died unexpectedly and I went to his funeral. We

were all – the actors who took part in *The House* and myself - deeply shocked by this loss, so we somehow felt that we needed to stage his novel *Brothers and Sisters*, the whole story without any cuts. Without going into more detail, I will just add that being a typical member of the intelligentsia, which generally incurs criticism these days, I didn't have the strength to refuse the offer any longer.

Have you ever had any regrets about it?

Almost immediately. We performed *The House* on the fortieth day after Abramov's funeral. I appeared on stage before the performance to say something and to ask the public to stand silently in his memory. As silence fell we suddenly heard the loud voices of two people arguing in the technical box. They didn't exactly swear but they were discussing their own problems very loudly and there was no way to stop them. So we spent the whole minute listening to them. I was traumatised. As I was leaving the theatre that night by the stage door, I passed some rubbish bins and thought "From now on, for the rest of my life I will have to deal with this crap. I won't, I don't want to". So in the morning I called them and said that I would have to turn down the offer, because I just felt that it would be the end of my directing career and that I would have to do things I didn't like doing. But the manager happened to be an intelligent man; he invited me in and we spent the whole day talking. So I stayed.

But I don't want you to think that I am complaining. This position was a real gift, because there I found a place where I could live the way which was right for me. As compensation for this freedom, I have to do some things I don't really like. And, like a sword of Damocles, I carry this constant fear of hearing coarse voices speaking in the silence about their trivial problems.

Do you remember the horrifying saying of Stanislavsky "The theatre is perishing!" I live with a constant feeling that we are on the brink of a collapse. I am not making the point that we don't have enough money, even if sometimes we don't have any at all. Every time the creative process is interrupted, it seems to me that everything will fall apart. And it could really happen. It takes ages to develop quality in art, but an epidemic of insanity spreads instantly.

When I see a toilet which has not been cleaned or a dirty floor where we are rehearsing, I become furious because it is a job which has been done without care and attention, and as a consequence everyone else can feel free to be careless in their turn. The longer you work the more difficult it gets; more and more questions arise, more "but"'s and contradictions. When I was young, directing a production was a very important thing but now it is different. "You've done another one - so what?" The most important thing is what you have learned and understood on the way. You approach each new project with more trepidation than the previous one.

They say that there are two types of directors - those who create a performance to change the world, and those who want to change something within themselves. Which type do you belong to?

I'm afraid it is hopeless to dream of changing anything in the external world. To try to understand something within ourselves is equally hopeless, but very tempting. That is why it is wrong to judge directors on their past work. We change and times change... Yesterday we spent the whole day rehearsing *The Cherry Orchard* which we have been performing for quite a while. The season is over so we don't have to work, but I have a list of questions for the actors and so we had another rehearsal. At first we thought we would just perform and talk, but we got so involved that we were rehearsing one and a half acts right up to midnight, interrupting and arguing.

I sometimes watch other directors insisting on their way of performing a scene, and I can see that they are happy to see their ideas realised. It doesn't bother them that these ideas may not have any ground or meaning. But their point of view is not the only possible one, and they haven't been blessed with infallibility. I remember how agonisingly difficult it was to rehearse the first act of Saltikov-Shchedrin's *The Golovlev Family* in the Moscow Arts Theatre. I started pacing around the auditorium, sat somewhere at the end of the back row to change my point of view... and all of a sudden everything became clearer. I had to leave this damned director's spot from which there is always only one point of view - literally one - physically and often also psychologically. That's why sometimes I

am even frightened to enter the auditorium and sit in the director's seat. I hear my deputy's cultivated voice: "Attention please everybody, the rehearsal has started" and suddenly I start feeling sick. If we don't follow this little ritual, I would probably make a fuss. I understand that all these small routines create a safe framework for our professional work. Otherwise you find yourself questioning everything, either switching the lights in the auditorium or suddenly jumping on the stage. I can understand why Stanislavsky sometimes asked for the furniture to be moved around the stage: he was trying to provoke both himself and his actors.

What are the distinctive features of an actor of the Maly Drama Theatre?

I hope that this type of actor might exist otherwise all our efforts would not be worth a brass farthing. We've been working together now for quite a long time and we have acquired some common perspectives. I can't say that we think alike - we probably have very different attitudes, but along the way we have shared some findings about human nature and human tragedy.

There is a whole system of training and, in essence, it is directed at enabling the actor to always relate himself to the time, the environment and the present moment of life. The important thing is to share what you gain from these surroundings; share it with your partners, not necessarily through speech, but through your own self, through your talents as an actor. When somebody – either actor or student – begins to tell me something, to describe something, I always stop them and say, 'Don't speak, just go and show me what you are feeling. This is your text, this is your work, you should just act and play what you feel.' We discovered that you can actually act everything; only you have to act yourself and not some imaginary figure whom you don't know. We try to become open to each other. In life many people can be very shy and even closed, and people often confuse freedom in life and freedom on stage. I have noticed that the freer the person feels himself in life, the more constrained he is on stage because probably a lot of his energy gets spent instead of being brought to the stage.

We recently introduced a new actor into an existing production, and we had a rehearsal because the introduction of this new arrival called for some changes. Paradoxically we ended up spending four days rehearsing with the actors who knew the play well. Initially I was surprised, but later felt quite happy about it since the arrival of the new actor had opened up new opportunities. All the actors started to see, hear and react in a different way and didn't mind working for hours to adapt their performance to the new person in the troupe. I don't believe this would have been possible with actors from another company. Putting it mildly, in another company, most probably, I would have faced a rebellion.

I rarely reprimand my actors about poor acting. First of all, I realise that it is partly my fault; secondly I know how difficult it is to act. And thirdly I know that all our actors want to act well and that they are doing their best. Lack of understanding or misinterpretation is something else, but it is not the result of someone's deliberate intention. I might say something harsh, but not very often. I understand more and more how hard it is to be an actor, how insane this activity is. And I understand more and more how hard it is to be a director…

There is a difference between an actor who simply speaks beautifully and one whose voice expresses the emotions he is experiencing; his hand makes the right gesture, his whole body speaks, so it's not all about articulating beautifully. Although very often on our stages you can see actors who have forgotten how to express themselves; they can neither speak nor make a wholesome gesture. This is the ABC of acting, and it is terrible when you see it disappear. The main thing is that our actors are constantly questioning, constantly searching. It doesn't mean that they are always enthusiastic about it. Sometimes it is not easy to engage them. Questioning always means being off balance and this might even be frightening. I once made some changes to a performance of *The Cherry Orchard* and saw that as a result it had lost some of its balancing points. Then I thought "What if they don't get them back?" But then I realised that we could do this and that: the possibilities were endless. I believe this is the most important aspect of our actors' capabilities. Deep inside, they

have an aptitude for it. I certainly hope so…

Perhaps I might be exaggerating. I know for sure that at rehearsals actors dream of acting in front of an audience and getting their share of applause. It is important for an actor to be assured that all his agony has not been in vain. The problem is that he can't see himself. That is the curse of his profession. Even a director can't see himself all that well: it takes time to start seeing yourself. The actor is like a man without a mirror. And yet the most fulfilling, the happiest moments of our profession come not from performing in front of an audience or from hearing their applause, but during our rehearsals. And what's more, they come during the difficult ones when it takes us ages to find solutions to our difficulties.

Do you generally enjoy rehearsals?

It's only during rehearsals that you have moments when you become free of your ego. You can reveal things that you would never normally articulate, and hear things which would not be normally spoken – this also happens in the confessional or in the moments of making love. You don't intentionally open up because, if you make a conscious effort, it wouldn't happen. It happens spontaneously and then you find yourself living on a different plane. I was with Abramov while he was finishing off his play *The House* and it seemed to me almost as though he was under the influence of a narcotic, although he never took any. We spent an hour in conversation during which time I could see how desperately he wanted to get back to his desk, because the words demanded to be put to paper.

One could call this "inspiration" but that sounds a bit pretentious, and I prefer to call it simply "effort". If anything ensures the survival of theatre, it must be this quality, because everything else conspires to destroy it, even so called "success". I don't really understand the word and don't like it, since nobody knows what success really means.

And which is your favourite project - is it the one you have just completed? Or is it the production you are currently working on?

God knows. Sometimes it's one and sometimes it's the other. So-

metimes the last one is the most excruciating because it doesn't allow you much relief. For instance, in St. Petersburg we had a few rehearsals of *Platonov*. Then we rehearsed it again in Weimar and put on eight or nine performances. I was worried during the first three and watched the subsequent ones, in the course of which I noticed many things which I thought were wrong, tedious and incoherent. Later, while I was on holiday, I mentally reconstructed the whole production, and back in the theatre we changed the second act almost entirely. Each production haunts me until I start a new one, as I am constantly seeking to add something to it. I rarely disengage myself from a production. I sometimes think my actors are happy when circumstances take me away and they aren't subjected to my direct supervision. It is also a very important stage when actors start to establish their own relationships and proportions. I watch them later and think "How inspired they are. How well they place themselves". But then again all of a sudden I start thinking, "They are getting too used to each other – too comfortable". It means that something needs to be done, so I become involved again.

How do you choose a particular play?
Sometimes the decision is immediate. This happened with *Platonov*. I wasn't able to put it on for another 25 years, but that's a different story. I decided at once that I wished to direct it, because my heart started racing at the idea. Yet sometimes it happens that I don't have all the actors I need for a particular play, and during the early years the company of course didn't exist.

But it is a jolt for me when I start reading the text. I remember how I spent a whole night reading volumes of Abramov's work – at that time his work was being criticised severely both because of his political views, and because of his supposed lack of artistic qualities. Though when I read him today, I see again how brilliantly he wrote. Recognition of true artistic worth comes only gradually. Artistic innovation occurs only rarely.

Whatever you read needs to be linked to your current state of mind. I once read Shakespeare's *Love's Labour's Lost* in Paris, which gave me the sense of a celebration of life. Ten days later when I came

home where there was no such ambience, all of a sudden I heard this play again and felt this desire for celebration. A profound experience stays with you for years. So at rehearsals you try to recall exactly what it was that made such an impression. In reality the staging of a performance itself is essentially a derivative activity. And the search for the scenographic form of it is purely a matter of technique.

Very often we work on a number of different productions at the same time. Actors under my direction are busy with one play, while my assistants are engaged on another with a different group of actors. From time to time we observe which project is progressing well, discuss it and decide that the time has come to concentrate on that particular production, and to leave the others to lie fallow for a while. For instance we spent a long time on Chekhov's *Three sisters*. When it was almost ready we realised that we hadn't found the question that Chekhov was asking with this play, and as for our own questions they didn't seem to be either interesting or stimulating.

The better the play, the more valuable it is. Chekhov's *The Cherry Orchard* is quite a conventional play in any sense, yet it's of absolute value for me. The key question however is how to get to the core of that value, how to penetrate into this perfect world, because Chekhov provides a perfect world, a perfectly created world. Of course it is relative, but a less perfect play is easier to get into. When we deal with masterpieces, they are completely closed in their perfection. If you can hear the music of a play and can relate to it, you feel related to your time and it means that you stand a chance of opening it up.

But even though it is a masterpiece, you have to create this play anew because only you can create a living experience. Then you begin to understand very simple things which are inside the play. A masterpiece can seem very complicated, but when you are penetrating into a play you begin to understand simple notions and simple things and when these simple words become your own words, the first steps have been made. It is a very long process; however much you respect a play, the process should be completely free because you won't get very far by having only great respect for the play.

Do you like your own productions?

Rarely. Sometimes it happens at rehearsals. Not at rehearsals of a forthcoming production, but of the current one. We have enjoyable rehearsals before the opening of a new season or while on tour. By then I am closely involved with my actors and they seem to be acting only for me. I love this moment when we perform only for each other. Recently I found it impossible to watch productions from the auditorium. Everything seems to be less subtle because of the audience and their reactions seem to lack refinement. So I find a place to view the production away from the audience. We have a little window from which I can watch unobserved…. When you stop talking to actors about their performance, they starts thinking that you've lost interest in them. So when I am not able to watch I have few trusted people who keep a record of the performance. But even when they use the right words and say good things it doesn't make me relax, or may be just for a second…

WHY I DON'T DIRECT COMEDIES

We feel the need to talk about things which concern us, because we seek after beauty and we perceive its existence. The tragic temperament of many artists of the 20th century originated from the schism between this quest and the reality of daily life. But if art loses this search for beauty, art becomes mundane.

However human awareness changes with the times. There are periods when evil seems to be in retreat, but later it returns and exacts its revenge. When we are confronted with evil, we feel as if good has ceased to exist anywhere.

Today at the beginning of the new millennium when we know so much about a human being and apparently put so much value on human dignity, we continue to eradicate human beings thoughtlessly.

I've seen children in Jerusalem escorted by people carrying machine-guns. They go to school laughing happily, yet tomorrow they may be dead. After an explosion caused by a Palestinian terrorist, I've seen human body parts falling on the theatre where my pupils were rehearsing. We have performed in Belgrade, not realising that we were only 140 km from Sarajevo. And people have cried while they watched *Claustrophobia* because a war was being fought and nobody wanted the war, but obviously they were not consulted. And as for our Chechnya...

It seems that human beings are programmed for self-destruction but this understanding doesn't help us feel any better. The Day of Judgement may be some way off in the future, but everything we see around us makes it seem as if it is already with us.

Sometimes things change for a short period. In post war Germany, for instance, a few generations grew up with a feeling of national guilt. But today this is starting to evaporate. "How long do we have to feel guilty?" say today's Germans, eager to cast off the virtue of redemption.

And we in Russia, with our famous "empathy with all humankind", refuse to admit any guilt and the fact that we too bear some responsibility. We try to find fault elsewhere - it's either the wrong policy or

the wrong leaders or even "the pernicious influence of the West" - but don't we also have blood on our hands? Don't our prisons, labour camps and civil wars proclaim our guilt too?

Art, as is well known, is a way of reflecting life, and it is one of the best ways of learning about what goes on in the human soul. Art speaks of what happens even if we try to ignore it, and first and foremost it speaks about pain: about human pain and suffering. It is the function of art to reflect society's pain. Principally art is uncompromising, dealing with uncomfortable and painful truths. Where there is harmony, there is less scope for art. In a perfect world art would fall silent, however paradoxical this might seem. While pain endures (as it always will), art will continue to search for whatever else exists in that pain. And it will always be unpleasant, always be awkward because it is not easy to become inured to pain, while listening to the testimony of art.

We will probably never understand whether death is an integral part of life, or life is merely a prelude to death. In any case remembering the boundaries of our existence makes us human, and compels us to be aware of life as Providence, recognising at the same time its original tragic nature. Sadly, during soviet times for decades we were taught not to think about death, and gradually we forgot also how to think about life. Life ceased to be cherished in our individual and collective awareness. In the context of the whole world the value of an individual human life is not great, but in our country its worth is infinitesimal. Sometimes it seems people live with no thought of death. It's frightening, because then anything is permitted. Dostoevsky wrote about this very issue.

Princess Diana's death aroused so much compassion and love, it gave me hope that not everything had been lost. But not long before her death a whole village in Algeria was massacred - almost 200 people - and the world press gave this brutal event barely a mention, while ours ignored it completely. Something in our consciousness and in our time has become distorted.

We merely act out the comedy of our existence, and if we feel too much despair, that's how life is. I feel no inclination to direct comedies. When we were young we had a lot of fun and produced many jocular performances. Those were dismal years, but we joked a lot and perhaps survived because of that. I think today also we have comic moments in our performances. But I am interested not in comic situations but in the amusement of self-recognition even when it is tinged with anguish.

I think that generally art can't be either purely dismal or cheerful. It deals with feelings. Today we might spread joy with our performance but tomorrow it may be impossible, so I try to convey something different. The important thing is I still want - in spite of everything - to talk, sing, scream or moan about something. Think of Dostoevsky. "What a depressing writer" many might say. But I say no; if a writer has the strength to talk about life's horrors and create something eternal out of them, it means that he is a great optimist. Dostoevsky depressing? He sees how frightful human nature is and still writes volumes about it. In his work he seems to think that it is impossible to change human nature, but as we read his novels we find that he believes in and hopes for something better. *The Possessed*, in spite of the implacable hopelessness of its analysis, is a ray of hope and it is impossible for spectators at our performances not to sense it. The more tragic and hopeless the action on stage, the more shocked and ultimately redeemed both the spectator and the actor feel.

That's how I remember Oleg Borisov acting in Dostoievsky's *A Gentle Creature* at the Moscow Arts Theatre. He spoke about human nature in severe and brutal terms, but the ability to speak about himself, to allow himself to experience it and open himself up with such passion, suddenly gave the audience some (even if illusory) hope.

I think that in such moments true theatre is born - when we feel empathy and instants of shared emotion and understanding, which is what we are intuitively constantly looking for.

In fact life is tragic in itself. Man is mortal and this is the principal tragic fact of his life, this burden of finality which he carries even at the moment he is brought into the world. It is born out of a desire to know ourselves, to know our relationship with the world and our own nature. By ignoring a man's origins and his life's purpose we have become merely physical beings, created without meaning. So we started to kill and destroy millions of people made in our own mould. I think this is the main catastrophe which has befallen us and our society.

Generally I hold a pessimistic view of life. I'm sure there is something ghastly in human nature, an inbuilt desire to destroy others similar to us… perhaps war is the easy way to evade our true nature, a way out from confronting our external and internal problems. We are preoccupied with solving all kinds of social and political problems, but the root cause of it all is human nature. Because it's not the system which makes people what they are, but people who determine the nature of the system. And sometimes it's necessary to protect a human not from the state, with its repression or discrimination, but from himself, from the evil within himself.

Art today, if it is to be worthy of the name, by definition should deal with the important problems of existence and not blindly follow current fashion. When it does, miracles happen, and people start thinking about matters they had forgotten in their preoccupation with everyday trivia. In being compassionate towards others, paradoxically they learn to be compassionate towards themselves; and not just to take pity on themselves but to observe, listen and think better.

Very few people have the capacity to surmount the hardships of their life. But when we do, we bring happiness to our nearest and dearest.

The chunks of pain and despair, which we put on the stage are our attempt at averting unpleasant events. But I have only a faint hope that theatre will change anything. Nevertheless this is our way of affirming our endurance, our hope.

Actually all disabilities are common to us all; they differ only in

their degree of familiarity and acuteness. The actor Oleg Dmitriev once told me that after a performance of *Claustrophobia* in France, a married couple approached him and asked how he knew so much about French husbands. In Russia we were often accused of vilifying the characters in our productions, but the French thought that the play was really about them... In truth art is about everybody. Everyone's life is hard and difficult.

Man is oppressed everywhere; even in the West he doesn't enjoy total freedom. People have problems with each other and with themselves. This is the cause of those flashes of aggression, which are restrained only by our civilised instincts; but civilisation is only a very flimsy veneer. That's why every manifestation of civilisation is so important. Theatre is still a sign of civilisation, even if an inadequate one.

When actors work intensively it can drain them of all their energy. A prominent newspaper critic once wrote "The time has passed when an artist suffered together with his own people; now he is fortunate enough to be able just to jot down passing thoughts and act them out". When I read this I nearly fell out of my chair in surprise, because in my opinion that is nonsense. Even in the prosperous West, art deals with the painful problems of human existence. Man is a tragic creature and he needs an art which is also tragic in nature. When we performed *Gaudeamus* in France, people came up to us afterwards and said "Our army is just as brutal as yours". A Frenchman knows when he's been oppressed and he doesn't care that somebody somewhere else might be oppressed ten times worse than him. As for us artists - we haven't moved to another country, we are still here where the same corruption, the same lies, cruelty and disrespect for human life continue to flourish. If we ignore all this, it means that we disregard our own humanity.

It seems to me that Europe today is oblivious to these moments of crisis which occur and to the dangers all around the world, even in the midst of Europe itself. We are used to the idea of "European civilisation", but in reality even a small occurrence is enough to fracture

the illusion. Civilisation and savagery are separated only by a very delicate barrier.

A character in a play set about the time of the Revolution says: "We don't have women's diseases now; all our diseases are shared." Now all the world's diseases are common to all of us.

Art today must make people feel on edge. It shouldn't insulate them from reality but instead make them experience something they can't experience in their everyday lives. Art exists to raise me up and appraise my life from a higher plane. At the end of a performance, or when I walk away from a painting or close a book, I am again brought back down to earth but the experience stays with me. Perhaps art doesn't liberate us from anything and doesn't change anything, but if we have managed to survive Auschwitz and the Gulags, we can thank art for that.

Man started acting as soon as he stood up on his hind paws. Even after an unsuccessful hunt or fight, he would later know success. Acting was a way of solving his problems, a way of evoking compassion for the one who hadn't won. And if he was successful, it was a method of self-affirmation, a way to understand the best of himself. In ancient Greece people spent days watching performances of wonderful stories, which today seem too sophisticated to many of us. Man hasn't become more intelligent and sophisticated today just because he has learned to master a computer.

Theatre, I think, is a biological need. You keep asking yourself what theatre is capable of. It is the same question as "What can a single person do when others are killed? When cruelty celebrates its victory, what can you do?" You can't stop it, but you can make people understand the main point - that we started off as primitive creatures but that we all have heads and hearts, and that it is a terrible sin to put an end to life.

Even when there is practically no reason for hope we make ourselves carry on hoping, because, if you deprive yourself of hope, only one thing is left - to do nothing and to admit that nothing really can be done. This is the most awful admission to make and renders your existence pointless. For whatever reason your actions

matter to someone. For whatever reason a person goes to a theatre, watches a performance, sheds tears... Even if it is just a tear, just for half a minute, it is still something. Perhaps he felt compassion for a prostitute wallowing in the mire. In real life no doubt he would pass by on the other side, but in the theatre he felt compassion. It's too naive to think that afterwards he would stop and stretch out his hand. But for this half a minute he was a human being in the fullest sense of the word. To spend an extra half a minute as a human - that's no bad thing. Generally in our lives only rarely do we manage to be truly human.

Pain is universal. Man is oppressed and humiliated everywhere, not just in Russia. And as soon as theatre rises up to meet the pain, the border has been crossed! We are really living in a crazy world. The main madness is the absurd prejudice that other people are formed in a different mould. Because of that people fight, humiliate each other and shed blood...

Theatre fights against this prejudice, at least by uniting people in the darkness of the hall. It unites them in compassion, in a common (even if momentary) pain. And this is already a miracle!

For us, for the people of theatre this is very important! Theatre really is a great idea, a great creation and a vital necessity for mankind.

After a performance only an instant of experience remains, nothing else. For some reason it continues to live on and doesn't die; that is the moment when something inside us remembered God.

The fact that theatre continues to live is a reason for hope. I think our work, whatever the impression it makes, shows our optimism, if I may use this word. Theatre is a constant search for perfection; it's an attempt to discover some harmony in the midst of the most terrible disharmony. This is its strength and courage. I think this kind of optimism is preferable to the contentment of those, who with eyes and ears shut, try to assure themselves that everything is all right

Sometimes we hear that theatre had one function during the Soviet era, another one during perestroika and a third one at present. I

think that this argument is absolute nonsense, invented by those who have only a very vague idea about theatre's specific character. In every age there is a need for a theatre which can drag people out of their mundane lives. We need a theatre in which it is not easy to immerse one self, and from which it is equally difficult to escape.

I am sometimes criticised about my passion for long performances. What can I do? I am sure that today's spectator needs to be dragged out of the routine of his everyday life for an extended period. A spectator who drops into the theatre after work needs to be shown that spiritually nothing will happen to him unless he leaves his superficial preoccupations behind and wishes to get immersed in the reality taking place on stage. For me today the ideal theatre is not one which fits easily into everyday life, but one which drags me out of it, creates doubt in me and demands fresh contemplation.

The role of the state in cultural development should be incomparably more significant. Unfortunately in recent years everybody has got used to the idea that theatre companies, as well as writers and artists should have to beg for resources. I think it should be the other way round: theatres should be asked to work and create something artistic. Until the state realises this, it will continue to decline, however great a power it might consider itself to be.

Perhaps the more unfavourable life is, the more productive art becomes, however depressing this may sound... In Russia we have little experience of a prosperous lifestyle, but our troubles help create an artistic impulse in us. We need to repeat this to ourselves because over these last years we have got used to saying that everything - culture, theatre and literature - have become worthless. But cultural life is still thriving in Russia and this is probably one of the few causes for optimism.

As dismal as it might sound I believe that the only thing which will prevent a general collapse in human relations is a constant effort at self-knowledge and a struggle to retain our values. For example, in

our theatre now the floors are polished, and for me even this apparently minor detail is a matter for celebration, no less than the occasion of a premiere. Our theatre is nice and clean today just as it used to be in the past. For me and for all of us, I believe, this is a matter of - please forgive the word - principle. It demonstrates our determination to keep on striving. We show this in the warm-up for rehearsal, in the rehearsal itself, in the discussions afterwards and in our performance on stage. It would be very easy to say that if our theatre is dirty and neglected, we actors don't need to put ourselves to any trouble either. If we have the opportunity to work, successfully or not is another question, we need to do our work properly. This is the only way to feel happy and fulfilled with what you do.

Ninety per cent of cultural institutions calling themselves theatres in fact have nothing to do with culture in my opinion. This is an exaggeration, of course, because even in a tedious performance you suddenly detect an affecting word or phrase, some genuine emotion. Sometimes I will be watching a performance I truly dislike - it's boring and I want to leave. But if I stay, at some point I suddenly notice that gradually I'm being drawn into the action on stage, especially if the play is not bad. By the end of the evening I don't regret having come, because I have picked up new ideas and enjoyed a fresh experience. What was the reason for that? Was it the company itself or the play which they didn't manage to spoil? It is not clear. But whatever it is, even untalented and unprofessional theatre doesn't do any harm. One way or another it deals with life and people. It doesn't kill people. I think that even the worst theatre is probably better than most other things. Moreover it changes a person's life, at least for an instant...

THEATRE – IT'S ALWAYS ABOUT MYSELF

At the dawn of humanity, primitive tribes performed dances in order to secure a good harvest, a successful hunt or a victorious ending to a battle with hostile neighbours. Thousands of years have passed since then, but man's desire to live other lives has remained undiminished. This is what theatre does for him.

I'm absolutely sure that people don't come to the theatre just to pass a pleasant evening. Whether they are aware of it or not, they come here to broaden their lives. Each performance shows them new facets of human experience. Sitting in an auditorium everybody can encounter both the highs of power, or the depths of an abyss.

Although the plot of a play is important, it is very much of secondary importance for the audience. They are gripped not by the plot, but by the passions portrayed on stage, which are in fact not all that varied. After all, man's life is very simple: he is born, he lives and loves and tries to procreate, to overcome his mortality. Whatever dramatists write about they, like novelists, finally concern themselves with these subjects. The spectacle of a dawn or sunset is also an integral part of our lives, which become extended each day by one dawn or shortened by one sunset.

But to entertain the audience is not theatre's main purpose, and I seriously believe this. Why does an artist, a talented one, of course, paint a picture? Because he finds it impossible not to paint. Why does a writer put pen to paper? Because he has to write. In the same way theatre creates a spectacle – to show something people care about. If we perform something that we think should concern others but leaves us (the actors) indifferent, we risk creating a piece that would fail to engage anyone. That's why we try to produce work which concerns us deeply, which we feel very personally.

This is my fundamental belief. It means for me that neither the function nor the essence of the theatre changes over the years in differing political situations or social upheavals. I am talking of course about true theatre, where people both on the stage and in the auditorium live out their lives fully.

Any performance is firstly about yourself. It doesn't matter in

which period or country the characters are set. Whatever you talk about, you always aim to talk about your own doubts and hopes; about what is happening or might happen to you; about what life does or might do to you.

I can never forget the productions of Anatoli Efros. What did they reveal to me? I learnt the truth about my country and about its social problems. But that and much more was revealed in passing. The main thing was that I learned about all the possibilities of human life and about life itself.

In his productions Efros was talking firstly about himself. That is why his theatre was genuine, among countless other false imitations. And his own deeply personal worries became equally personal for thousands of other people.

In the list of rules for the actors of the Commedia dell'arte the following was written: fear nothing and don't ponder. Of course it didn't intend to encourage simple thoughtlessness. In reality it meant: not to fear responsibility, not to fear being different, not to fear the reactions of the audience... It's a pity many of these rules have been forgotten now. I think that the reason classical theatre survived was that it was too busy solving the essential problems of its era to be bothered with the individual. Tens of thousands of spectators had come to the amphitheatre, and it was impossible to worry about each individual - it had to solve fundamental problems...

I can't say that we necessarily follow the same path: that would sound too self-assured. But we honestly don't worry about who, other than ourselves, is likely to find our performances interesting. Whatever is of real importance to one person is likely to be of concern to many others. People come to the theatre to see stories which engage them. *The Possessed* is a spectacle which runs for ten hours. Nobody would ordinarily tolerate a ten hour performance to watch a story about the development of some revolutionary movement or even about Dostoevsky's prophecies. But they would be prepared to spend even 20 hours to learn something about themselves. And if this self-knowledge becomes the main thing then everything will work out well... It's easy to say this, but much more difficult to create.

Our performances contain bits and pieces of our lives, and the life of another person helps you to understand your own. That is why, when in a casual conversation somebody talks to us about their problems, we interrupt them to tell them about ours. It is not because we are uninterested in other people's concerns, but because by sharing we feel that we are all affected in the same way... This is a very typical moment in theatre, based on common human experience.

I think that genuine theatre is always poetic. People often think of poetry as being just sentimental couplets about beautiful landscapes, but poetry is life in concentrated form. Lyric poetry is not about love, as people might often think; it is about our inner life as individuals. I think that our theatre is incredibly lyrical. We deal in our performances with happiness and suffering, hopes and illusions. If you put on a performance with other people's reaction in mind, somehow, imperceptibly, insincerity starts to creep in. In worrying about other people's perceptions, you start imagining that they are different from your own.

I hadn't been to Italy before seeing the films of Fellini and never imagined that I would ever go there with our company. But without having even visited Italy, we found that we understood everything in his films - not about his characters, but about ourselves. For example I remember so vividly my astonishment, while watching *Amarcord*, the feeling that the film was about *my* youth and how it was impossible to portray it more accurately than Fellini did. Although there was no event in the film corresponding directly to my childhood, in its own way it was about my boyhood.

English audiences laugh often and loud. The Japanese in contrast laugh less and more quietly, although they say afterwards "I rolled about with laughter". That is the only difference. All spectators however cry at the same parts of the performance; except that some cry more openly while others just shed a tear. It doesn't happen that in one country people will cry at one place and in another they will laugh at the same part. People cry or laugh for the same reason whe-

rever they are from. That is the power of serious theatre; it arouses emotions which are universal. We sometimes think that a play about our own lives might not be interesting for non- Russians. But we have performed Ludmila Petrushevskaya's *The Moscow Choir* in many countries. The plot seems so quintessentially Russian - about life in a soviet communal block of flats - but it's really only the story of a family with their joys and sorrows. Communal life is familiar to everyone, since it takes place not only in apartment blocks but also within families. In fact human problems are much more universal than we realise, we just try to persuade ourselves that we are different.

Bringing together people and generations is perhaps the purpose of culture. When it fails to do so, our whole life starts to break down. Thanks to these cultural links humanity has been living for millennia, and surviving, in spite of all the turmoil. Not without reason every new civilisation had to recreate these links from scratch. Even the dances of primitive people were nothing but a cultural link. Theatre is an art that from ancient times has actively created an internal human harmony. It needs buildings, a stage and equipment, but even these are not essential. All that is required is a couple of actors and a surface to stand on. A building can be destroyed, but people would still be able to create fantasies on the eternal questions: What if I love you? What if he doesn't? What if he hates me? What if I don't?

A genuine theatre is always about us human beings. There isn't a single person who doesn't have lost illusions and failed hopes and fears; things which hamper their freedom of movement and spirit. Nobody is inured to humiliation, even those who are well off. If they laugh and cry at performances, it is because they recognise themselves on stage.

Evidently western Europeans live much more balanced and comfortable lives than we do in Russia, however they still have their own problems. And the longer you live there, the more you understand

why. The intensity of their problems might vary but in essence they are the same. Even if we say "It's their comfortable lifestyle that makes them so fussy" for them it is still an affliction or inconvenience. When, after a performance of *Gaudeamus* in England or in France, the audience says that they have the same problems in their armed forces, we know well that they are not really "the same". But since an army is an instrument of suppression, even in their army people feel humiliated, although perhaps in a more civilised way. But for each person his own humiliation is the most important and the most painful one... Humiliation, neglect, unhappy love, professional failure etc... Our own problems are everybody's, because the things that move us are universal. When I put on a play I think of what moves me, and what moves those acting in it. What happens to me? What happens to them? How do my emotions relate to theirs? That is all. Whether it will provoke dead silence or bursts of laughter, we have to wait for our audience to find out.

1991 was not exactly a year when one would have thought of putting on a production lasting ten hours. The making of The *Possessed* was truly challenging: these were the years when people didn't have enough food, but still kept coming to our performances, sometimes with their boiled potatoes because that was all they could afford. We discovered that even hunger is no obstacle to spending ten hours with Dostoevsky; quite the contrary. We should rely on our intuition and do what we find genuinely interesting, otherwise we end up making fools of ourselves.

The idea of performing all three parts of *The Possessed* on the same day came to us because we didn't want to interrupt the whole experience, neither for ourselves nor for the spectators. In Braunschweig we performed it once in one day and another time spread over three evenings. It became clear that the former was much better. After completing the first part the actors were only stopping reluctantly. They had started something which they found very difficult to pick up again the following day. I think that for the audience it was the same. With the one day performance they were experiencing a sort of spiritual adventure; a whole day in the theatre with Dostoevsky. If

they stayed, it meant the performance took on a life of its own and I think that is very important. In spite of the revolutions we have lived through, our everyday lives are filled with irritation and malice and it becomes especially important to show that such an undertaking is possible. Of course there were objections and we would be asked: "Who would come to the theatre for a whole day?" But it turned out that there were many 'crazy' people prepared for such an adventure. There is a great need for spirituality everywhere; it is not our prerogative. The idea about Russian spiritual superiority is just a myth; there are many cultures which are open to this. I think people involved in theatre should have the confidence to take risks; there would be many people ready to respond.

The impresarios everywhere in the world are trying to find something new but end up producing something familiar. They are afraid that their audience would stay away; it is easier to sell something that the audience recognises. Producers always underestimate their audience and this obliges directors to put on again what they performed yesterday. In truth audiences don't know what they want to see. Directors need to be bold enough to believe that they know what the public would enjoy seeing.

There is no way of knowing how the audience will respond to our words. We can't a priori divide spectators into those who will and those who will not understand. Very often people don't know what they are capable of or what would they like. Josef Brodsky wrote in one of his articles that in art it is not demand that provides supply. Quite the opposite: only supply can develop demand.

We perform for very different audiences. The reaction doesn't depend on whether they are educated or not - sometimes education makes it more difficult. In theatre it is better to forget about comparisons. Theatre is like love. You mustn't be tense, otherwise you can't enjoy it. That's why I sometimes even prefer a spectator who could honestly say that they haven't read Dostoevsky.

A person might not appreciate some layers of the performance but I am sure they will respond to the core of it if the performance has achieved its main goal - to awaken the emotions. The biggest pro-

blem today, among all our big problems, is the loss of the right to emotions. Sometimes we feel we don't have them at all: life is fast and mechanical; TV constantly bombards us with materialistic images which target our baser needs...But in fact man remains the way he was created and his heart is unchanged. And that's what makes him human - the ability to get shaken up by the experiences of others. Theatre makes people think of themselves through the experiences of others. It doesn't happen that often in real life, so theatre momentarily brings us back to ourselves.

We should listen to ourselves and be true to ourselves. Play our own music again and again. Obviously we are happy when somebody sings along with us or sheds a tear at our sorrow... I am a pessimist and I know that theatre can't do much. But I am also an optimist, since I believe: theatre can do something.

WHY DOES A DIRECTOR NEED HIS OWN COMPANY?

Any book, any printed word we habitually call literature although there is literature, there is fiction and there is pulp fiction. And if today we are beginning to feel that the theatre of like-minded people and the aesthetic and ethics attached to it have lost their meaning, it just shows that in the world of theatre things have gone wrong; that fundamental truths on which scenic art, especially in Russia, has always been based are being forgotten. It shows that instead of being art theatre has become something like fiction or even pulp fiction.

Any good concepts become overgrown with false interpretations if used too much. To somebody "like-minded people" might mean "people thinking the same way"; or some might even joke: "people who have just one thought". Let the former have their prejudice, and the latter - their jokes. "Like-mindedness" in Russian culture has always meant sharing the same faith, sharing a belief in the existence of some spiritual truth. A search for this truth involves sacrifices and self-denial as in any faith. And finally it involves human community as it is impossible to find this truth on your own.

Since we are talking about ensemble theatre the result of this search will be expressed in a role, a performance etc., but everything is based on a spiritual substance. That is why a group of actors with little experience who get together with the intention of producing a 'sensational show' in order to 'rub everybody's nose' cannot be considered 'like-minded, neither are they an 'ensemble'. Ambition is not a ground for like-mindedness. The spiritual foundation gives the opportunity to suppress an actor's vanity, professional egotism or mercantilism. If they manage to suppress it for a long time, a performance is being born, if just for a while – a good role or scene materialises.

I am convinced that in the creation of any performance marked with a spark of talent there has been a moment when all the participants felt that the making of it was the most important thing in their lives. This naive maximalism does not provide achievement but makes it possible.

I don't like to criticise anything; least of all an artistic effort, because you never know where you will find a real pearl. But in general the idea of commercial enterprise in the theatre is alien to me. It is a commonplace but Stanislavsky's main book is called "My life in Art" exactly because art cannot exist without the 'life in it'. The theatre of one show is almost always theatre-factory where the main idea is to win at any cost and this is an idea more suited to sport. It is easier to win by always doing the same thing and that is how the mythology of stars came to live. The concept of 'a star' is very different from the concept of an artist, because an artist is someone who searches for the unknown. And a star is somebody who has already found it and wants to keep it. The 'star' has to constantly shine with what has made them a 'star' in the first place. They can't change because no one would forgive them. Theatre performance should have a long life and develop over a period of time. But commercial productions are a disposable thing, like disposable plastic plates. I don't like plastic plates, although they say they are very hygienic. But art and hygiene are two different things.

Any serious performance in any theatre is created in an atmosphere of collective research. Only spiritual community can bring to life the potency of the collective artist. Everything that divided, antagonised or irritated the troupe gives way for a while. When the collective artist is at work the performance is always good.

The idea of theatre as a home is deeply rooted in Russian theatre. It is another matter that 'home' can easily become 'broken home'. It depends on the family which inhabits it. If I know that my production will last just for a few weeks I am not sure I would want to do it. Theatre is already a ephemeral occupation, so how could we face planning our baby's death?

I defend theatre as an artistic whole. Repertory theatres exist all over the world but the term repertoire has begun to mean something different. Obviously it is preferable to the one show-theatres but it's not ideal because the principles of commercial theatre have still been applied: a company is created for every performance, the number of rehearsals is fixed and the lifespan of the production is limited. No

wonder now they use the term "production" instead of the French "spectacle". Theatre is transformed into a factory and the shows are quickly produced, quickly used and quickly forgotten This is not art because art aspires to eternity.

That's why I think that Stanislavsky's model is ideal. Even if a company doesn't manage to become a 'home' to the actors, they are still united in many ways and still have the opportunity to create.

I am so passionate about this model, despite the fact that this 'home' could become dysfunctional, violent or unloving, because it has the capacity to reinvigorate art. It's like a family. It gives an opportunity to love, to have children, to bring them up. Going to a system of casual liaisons won't do any good. Brook, Strehler and Bergman spent a lot of time working in other theatres but created their main works at home, within their permanent companies. They all gravitate to the Russian model. The iron system of commercial theatre is impossible to destroy. However, actors in the West are prepared to fight for subsidising of companies and not of a single production; for the process of work and not just the result. It is amazing how much money is spent on festivals and theatre buildings all over the world but how little anybody cares for the normal life of actors, for the good conditions at rehearsal. Process is something you can't touch with your fingers, and if it can't be touched it can't be subsidised. Art is immaterial. Festivals and tours don't define the life of a national theatre.

The nightmare of every permanent theatre company is getting overgrown with cliché. The cliché can be overcome only within the company. A theatre of stars doesn't need to do this since it is based on cliche and is valued for that. The ideal theatre would have a varied repertoire of plays, but not as it used to be in the Soviet era: we were obliged to produce one Soviet, one Russian and one Western play. And unlike in a Western theatre where they are given a month for rehearsals, a month for the run and then a month for the next play... Each spectacle is a chunk of life and a varied program of plays gives a fuller picture of life...

I can say as much against the permanent company as I said in its defence. It has lots of negative aspects: stagnated perceptions, hie-

rarchy, annoying ambitions. I hate 'ordinary' theatre. That was the reason Stanislavsky wrote "Watch out!" soon after the Moscow Arts Theatre was formed. But in that theatre it was still possible to scream "Watch out!" and hope that someone would hear. There are places where it's more like a desert – screaming or not won't make any difference.

Obviously in a theatre where you have to work with actors whom you've only just met, even if they are very professional, it is difficult to achieve spiritual community or even find a foundation for it.

Ages ago in the unfamiliar for me then Maly Drama Theatre I was rehearsing Capek's *The Robber*. Things were not coming together and I was desperate that nobody understood me and, what was more important, didn't want to understand me. Then Nikolay Lavrov joined the theatre, I had worked with him before in YVT and I had even read some lectures on his course. We understood each other and shared a common language and memories. The associations I made meant something to him and his views were important for me. One role, the role of the professor played by Lavrov, started to emerge.

Talent has to be seen to be believed; spiritual community has to be felt to be trusted. It is contagious and soon all the other actors wanted to be part of it. The whole atmosphere started to change. It was a very uneven performance and the audience didn't accept it unanimously, but the 'infection' of like-mindedness had already spread. That is why *The Robber* was very dear to me and actors loved to perform it year after year.

In any case it was much easier to fulfil my next idea and actors began to believe that our search might give them the answers to many of their questions. Nevertheless the beginning of our work on Abramov's *The House* was very painful and all the problems came back. Disbelief and unwillingness to explore the material exploded with a new strength. If it had not been for that bit of 'infection' of like-mindedness that we had experienced with *The Robert*, and for the support of the same Lavrov and Sergey Bahterev, Tatyana Shestakova, Igor Ivanov, who were all my pupils in different years, we

wouldn't have succeeded and there wouldn't be a Maly Drama Theatre today.

When you succeed in creating something good outside your company it's always like a miracle. Had Oleg Borisov not been in the Bolshoy Drama Theatre, and Innokenti Smoktunovsky and Ekaterina Vasilieva in the Moscow Arts Theatre, I don't know how I would have finished my experiments. I was able to work with these actors because we managed to achieve, even temporarily, even if in the space of that particular performance, a sense of ensemble.

When I was young it seemed to me that anything can be done in any theatre. The main thing was to "solve" that scene or the other. "Finding a solution" for the scene or the performance was like having a magic wand, it was the mantra of all theatre directors. Now I know: there is nothing more important than human substance. Theatre is a collective art. And it needs the soul of a collective artist.

There is a theatre the forms of life of which have been discovered by Stanislavsky. At the core of this brilliant discovery is the possibility of the collective artist (although "collective" has become a negative word today), the possibility of spiritual community (although we don't like the word "spiritual" either). According to Stanislavsky theatre is a spiritual, living entity: that's what it is. It is a group of people who are united not only by their performance on stage but also by shared ideas, values or simply by shared joys and misfortunes... Those who criticise ensemble theatre don't understand that the number of years people spend together provides that complex human experience that is so absorbing to watch and that could be never achieved in a quickly created commercial show.

In the director's relationship with the actors everything should come naturally, like in life. Any artificial creation is dangerous; any violence is dangerous. I believe that things should be left to flow in a natural way. There is a popular belief that actors are not the brightest of people: of course it's easier to work with the most talented and intelligent ones. It is easier to involve talent in co-creation and intelligence in co-thinking; lesser efforts are needed to awaken actors for the work.

It seems to me that we never treasure enough the studio conditions we have created in our theatre, the notion that this is our work laboratory. It is important to have good relationships, but we do not have to be intimate friends with everybody. We don't have to clutter our everyday life with constant declarations of love and vows of like-mindedness. I have experienced that kind of relationship in one theatre and I know very well what it is like: it is a rather unpleasant thing.

To lose their inhibitions and feel comfortable at rehearsals actors need an utmost independence. That is why we've created little rituals in our rehearsals; they allow a special space to be formed where people feel free to say and do what they wouldn't dare saying or doing anywhere else. I know it from my own experience. An enormous inner culture, discipline and tact are needed to gain the right to feel boundless freedom at the important moment when you need it in your performance. Interference in people's spiritual lives is a tyranny. It is pointless to impose a false sense of community and I think that in art like in church and in life, it is a despicable lie that only make things worse.

The everyday life of a theatre is woven from little things and instants of greatness very rarely appear. Sometimes they emerge at rehearsals but immediately fade away. That is how theatre exists – by repeating the same things year after year, performance after performance. Sooner or later a moment comes when the staff - technicians, actors, managers begin to feel tired and ask: "when is this going to finish? We want to do something different!" I have noticed that the actor who has not been criticised or praised often enough and has not been told whether he's good or bad in today's or yesterday's performance eventually gets weaker and begins to lose his confidence. He starts doubting his acting ability and begins to think that it doesn't matter much to anybody. This is typical not only for actors but for everybody in the profession. Each of us needs to know how our work affects other people. In this sense theatre is a very exact model of life but in a more concentrated and rather naive form. Naive because, fortunately, in theatre people don't get killed and mar-

kets don't collapse for real. If there is rivalry it is a sacred one - rivalry over roles and competition for better work. In our theatre, of course, even the props man competes with his colleague secretly thinking that he's better at his job. Everybody feels very special. But that's what makes life in theatre and in particular in the Maly, so exciting: it is a notch above reality.

The theatre I am trying to work in is a theatre that unites people, that helps them to relate to each other. I am not a madman or a fanatic to demand boundless service to the altar of art. But there is something which is more important to us than success, applause, fame etc. The searching and learning together - those are the moments that bring us sheer delight. The joy comes not from finding something but from searching well... To us theatre is part of life, an extension of life and perhaps bigger than life.

A THEATRE OF PROCESS, A THEATRE OF RESULTS

There are two ways of approaching the work: you can either concentrate on the presentation of the material or immerse yourself into its exploration. The first way leads, at best, to a good quality performance. The second one leads to the birth of a "new reality". Perhaps the first way is also worthy and professional. But you always dream of the second one, then every rehearsal becomes an exploration, a search...

Exploring different versions of the same thing is important to me in principle. Before deciding on a scene, movement or gesture we have to find out the most accurate version of that character's behaviour. We start by highlighting certain aspects, exploring new circumstances or recreating moments preceeding the scene. We call the process probing and the bits we create – probes. We could perhaps call them etudes or studies, but the majority of theatre terms are so overused, it is better to invent your own. By varying the circumstances in which our characters act gradually we arrive at the only true inner motif, that is valid for this particular character in this particular situation. Sometimes, we choose at the end the one that we have found in our very first probe, but our search was not in vain. Formally the solution remained the same but through our elliptic search it has changed in quality: our probe has acquired texture and dimension.

I must say that probing is essential to any artist. The process of probing can be very messy and time has to be allocated for this. Actors must have a right to make mistakes or to fail in several probes. These failures are an inseparable part of the exploration of life that will be presented in that production. The actor's freedom in this process; his belief that the process is more important than the result; that the purpose of the probe is not to act well but to find something true in the material and in themselves: I think, all these are necessary conditions of the working process.

We often speak about the importance of creating a 'second plan' for the character. In fact many actors can easily do it. But we forget that according to Stanislavsky this 'second plan' must encompass the whole life of our hero. You need time for this knowledge to build up.

That's why we need numerous probes, discussions, observations: everything that allows us to place ourselves in a broad psychological and aesthetic context. Usually this part of the working process is completely overlooked but there is nothing that can later replace it. There is never enough time, but I am convinced that the time dedicated to this process is rewarded in full.

Once the actors have at their disposal the whole emotional palette of the character and the play, it is easier for them to act out their parts in any circumstances. Only then that unique state occurs that Stanislavsky called: "I am". The problem of embodying the role doesn't exist anymore. "I understand" becomes equivalent to "I am" or "I live". The process of creating a performance is not like laying bricks but more like giving birth: all the elements have to work organically.

I immerse myself in the material of the play (or life) without knowing what the final result will be. I can only guess it, search for it, explore it. Otherwise I can go straight for the result cutting corners, choosing the shortest route. The first approach is not recommended in commercial theatre. Today's theatre is preoccupied with the audience's perceptions and has completely succumbed to it. Serious artists work in conflict with the audience's expectations, they aspire to discover the unknown, while commercial artists tend to reproduce what was already there.

The expressions "well staged play" or "well acted performance" have always been synonymous with craftsmanship. But today they are emerging as measures of artistic value. Gradually basic values are being replaced. For me one of the most serious problems for theatre today is to avoid becoming merely a factory churning out performances, even if they are eye catching and sensational, and being in essence a creative organism. There is a universal danger of mere imitation of creative work. The total dedication to the rehearsing process, which was Stanislavsky's central concern, has become a rarity.

The act of creation is a deep and serious psycho-physical process and it can occur only in certain conditions. Every director finds their own way to create them. The main thing is to engage in a producti-

ve way the deepest forces of the human being. The theatre of organic life is directly open to human nature, using it both as material and purpose of creativity.

Some actors think that a role can be created within three hours of rehearsal. What a delusion! That time won't be enough to create a single gesture. The creation of something new is possible only as a result of a detailed creative exploration. Styles and aesthetics change but the essence of creating in theatre remains the same.

If the definition of a strong director today is somebody who is capable of staging a production in a short period of time, I prefer to be in the group of the not so strong ones.

Before starting rehearsals the full content of the material has not opened up yet. We can only discuss it, study it, penetrate it. The right to this content has to be earned through persistent enquiry. Only then can it be transformed into a worthy piece of theatre: not a mere plot retold but a piece of real life theatre. I prefer not to formulate the main task in advance: any formula invented before the start of rehearsals would restrict the work.On the other hand, progress isn't be possible without a helm and sails: one must have a clear notion of the main thought, the main mood, the main line of action. For instance, I try not to start rehearsals before the set is ready. The work on the set is also a phase in the process of learning. For a very long time I don't talk with designers about shapes or colours; we just discuss what we see in the play, sometimes we even write down some themes making a catalogue of our sensations to stimulate each other… I am convinced that the set, like each role, like the whole performance, mustn't be 'planned' or 'constructed' but has to evolve.

When I was working on Dostoevsky's *A Gentle Creature* very early on we had a feeling that in fact it was a liturgy: a liturgy which takes place in a half-empty, dingy flat in a large St. Petersburg block with an inner courtyard open to the never ending northern sky. By connecting all these elements - the flat, the yard, St. Petersburg, the endless sky – Eduard Kochergin created a special space for this performance – an azure grimy temple of solitude, closed off from everything else, but also easily transformed into a street; the wall was going straight up towards the ceiling or perhaps towards the sky…

I am not going to describe Kochergin's work in detail here; I will only say that in my opinion he expressed with remarkable accuracy what I would call a liturgical beginning. But the word "liturgy" itself came up at the rehearsals much later. I dared to pronounce it only when I was certain that it would describe for the actors what they already felt in themselves.

This is not a trick to lead actors to what you as director have already decided. By working with them I set myself as director on a completely new track that might take me far away from my preliminary impulses and sensations. In rare cases, when your initial idea had happened to be truly organic, there is a chance that in the end you will come back to the thoughts you have started with. The conception has to be in essence a product of the working process. The process of birth and realisation of the performance is also the process of the birth and realisation of its concept. These two processes are united and inseparable but they develop in parallel.

To be honest we never intentionally look for new material: there are so many wonderful books and plays around. More often we start with what excites or worries us. That is what you try to understand with the actors during rehearsals: the reasons for our own reactions to that material, and we try to express what we have found in the language of theatre. We spent several years working on *Platonov* for example. Why? Because life changes but the essence of human tragedy stays the same and we found ourselves absorbed by this.

The process is the primal thing – we forget this unique thesis of Stanislavsky. On the other hand, the process doesn't guarantee a satisfactory result: we don't know what will come out of it. A good, serious performance is as unpredictable a miracle as a great book or great piece of music. Success that is easily repeated is something rather suspicious. I can't say that I accept failure easily. Of course I worry and agonise and lose sleep, but nevertheless I always know that we can win with a failure and this is sometimes less scary than to endure a success.

I think we talk too often about the "fast flow" and "fast rhythm" of

modern life. Theatre is really beginning to adjust to them, but in doing so it stops being what it should be. Today life superficially fizzes and seethes, but at a deeper level there are complicated social and spiritual processes at work. It is more important than ever before to analyse this deeper layer. The more dynamic life is the more serious, calm and worthy theatre should become. In an era of fast changes an artist needs to think more slowly. It is no mere chance that today theatre has sunk to the level of a chat show and popular entertainment. Kenneth Tynan said that every serious work of art must be a bit boring. A serious book is by no means a light and captivating read. The type of "captivating theatre" which has established itself today could lead us far away from the real purposes of art.

When you are young life seems to be endless. At some point it starts getting more packed with things and you begin to feel that you and the time follow different tracks. Everything becomes more fast and intense. You want to catch up but you don't want to rush; you feel that you have to and the constant pressure makes you anxious. The same applies in theatre. We try not to hurry and dwell on details. But because there is so much to get through, we hasten. That's why sometimes I am so happy at rehearsals - it's a kind of suspended time.

We are generally a very disciplined company but at rehearsals the atmosphere is easy going… I think that the rules should be strict but there is no harm in loosening up sometimes. Rules and rituals provide some structure to our life. But every ritual starts to become an obstruction when you get too accustomed to it, and you feel the need to break free from it.

In a company general rules and a reasonably high level of organisation are needed; in order to get from Paris to Milan, 110 people must arrive punctually at the coach and at the airport. Nothing can be done without regard to time - the same principle applies to theatre. We get our principal skills not from regulation but from rehearsals. Rehearsals require genuine dedication. Long practice and training create attitude to pressures that eventually leads to personal freedom. Sometimes you might come to the rehearsal feeling

unwell but the other actors come prepared, and you have to get up and get involved and feel the joy of being able to do it…Nobody wants to be bad at what they do but if they fail to notice how obvious it is to the others and can't admit their own fault they can very quickly become cynical – they say to themselves that nobody cares or it won't make any difference, and this is a dangerous path to take for any actor…

Rehearsals and everything else to do with the creation of a performance completely dominate the lives of actors and directors. I'm convinced that every actor is imbued with a special power which gives him millions of unexplored possibilities. And these possibilities (as with the law of gravity) settle in the depths of their spirit and do not easily rise to the surface. Huge efforts are required to uncover them. That's why rehearsals in our company are such a frantic process; for me too it's acutely interesting. Rehearsals kindle a belief in us that through them our lives are somehow changed. It's like prayer. A man prays out of faith and this faith becomes more important than anything else. Yes, we know millions of prayers don't change anything, but faith nevertheless endures.

During rehearsals you detach yourself from your everyday life and cast off your inhibitions and somehow something emerges. It may be something that you want to expel but it is also a chance to express yourself to your fullest extent. Each rehearsal should be unique to ensure that actors or students would be worried about missing the next one. Every time they have to be shaken up and somewhat disorientated. It's a bit like arriving at a new place – at first you lose your bearings but then start to get acclimatised. We need a speck of uncertainty which will stop us saying: "That's the way I want it done". We have a tendency to rest on our laurels, a fantastic ability to relax totally. If you don't berate actors at rehearsals they won't have anything to occupy their minds until the next one. If you say "That's really good", the tension evaporates.

We are often dissatisfied with ourselves. It is because we seek perfection, and it is unachievable. We seek after the truth and that is unattainable too. All we are left with is constant effort, probing. In

our company we don't say: "I'm rehearsing". Instead we say "I'm probing"; not "he or she acted well" but "his probe was good". In fact we rarely say the word "good", we say "it makes sense" instead - it describes our sensation of what we are doing better. Whenever we return to *Brothers and Sisters*, we could perform it just as we did before but we know that we could make it better. It all requires training and practice of course, and also we need confidence in the necessity and truthfulness of what we are doing. And that is what we do every time. One would say, if it was OK why change it? It might have been OK but you are never sure...

In the West they work differently. They decide on something, then stick to it. They have taught themselves to work this way – their settled lives have taught them to follow this method. If that is their way, then so be it. I can't be sure that our way would be more fulfilling...However they are starting to appreciate our approach. They feel that it liberates something in them...

Meyerhold used to say that the premiere is the first step in the decay of the production, unless of course we constantly allow the possibility of development. Stanislavsky meant much the same thing when he said that there is a "theatre with notes" after each performance, and a "theatre without notes"...

At the start of the new season we rehearsed *The House*. We must have performed it more than fifty times, and yet the rehearsal still lasted five hours and we managed to get through only a few of the scenes, finding things we had not previously noticed. Not a single mise en scene was altered but many nuances of the characters inner lives became sharper and more thorough.

On every tour we rehearse the play which we are going to perform. It's almost always one or two full runs of the play with discussions and comments. Every performance on tour in fact becomes a premiere. Before the start of the tour superlatives can be written in the media about you; however the audience isn't much interested in that as the advertising won't necessarily convince them to buy tickets. When people come to the theatre they come to watch a unique event. In Lille nobody cares that the previous audience in Toulouse

gave us a standing ovation. At every performance we need to create something fresh to win them over. It helps to keep us in shape and gives us confidence. It's so easy to lose your confidence and your trust in your own artistic necessity.

The more that kind of spontaneity is injected into a performance, the longer the production will live on. It doesn't repeat itself but takes on a life of its own and develops like a living organism. I measure the life of a production in years, not days. A performance could mature, get more intelligent. It changes regardless of what we want. It is especially obvious when it's done over many years by the same group of actors. *Brothers and Sisters* has been in our repertoire for 18 years and the majority of the performers haven't changed. That is what makes a performance unique.

Maeterlink's *Blue Bird* was running at the Moscow Arts Theatre for a few decades but they kept changing the actors and that is slightly different. When a production is played by the same cast, it becomes imbued with a special quality. People change, something happens to them and this 'current of life' flows through the performance too… Our performances, if they work, they cling to life. There is always some inner freedom, an ability to breathe differently and move on in some direction. I'm not talking about the mise en scene or the external curve of a role but the inner net of a performance. Over many years people become more subtle. They hear more and develop more empathy both in life and on the stage. That is why performances become more acute, profound and subtle if they develop along human lines.

When rehearsing we try to understand firstly something about ourselves. This knowledge is very fragile. That is why theatre is such an endless pursuit. Something constantly changes within ourselves and the world and your relationships with it changes too and this is one of the most absorbing things to watch. In essence we might say we don't 'make performances' but endlessly explore ourselves.

Theatre is the only thing I can do, it's a physiological necessity, a kind of appetite for life. I am tormented by the feeling that life is so

short, narrow and limited but at rehearsals you live out the most interesting moments of your life. You can realise this only in the theatre. Only at a rehearsal, having shut yourself off the rest of the world, can you actually live another life!

And that's why over the years we get less interested with results and more with the process. We like our own performances less and less and don't look forward to the first night because what we've been living out for months turns out to be a result, one which others might reject. I think that the spectator most of all wants to live through that experience of ours!

As for me a theatre without astonishment, without emotions is no theatre at all, however intellectual it might be. I am less and less attracted by stage effects, flashy mise en scenes and all. In theatre the main effects must be the human passions. Nor am I a fan of grand spectacles. While I was directing Tchaikovsky's opera *The Queen of Spades* in Paris, they were also showing Rameau's *Les Indes Galantes*, a show which required hundreds of costumes. I would be happy with only three as long as the audience's emotions were engaged.

MIRACLES MADE TO ORDER

I have always believed in the importance of the simple things in life, such as wonder at the sun's rays or the creation of a snowflake.

One person is amazed at seeing an apple fall from a tree and goes on to discover the law of gravity. While another, observing tiny changes in nature expresses it in poetry, like Boris Pasternak, or yet another survives the process of growing up and plays Hamlet, like Paul Scofield. It is a disaster when all this wonder vanishes and sensitivity is eradicated. Why does it happen? The devil knows!

People, who don't use their talent professionally, never lose it; only if they lived a very harsh life. I once knew a wonderful old woman, who in 1953, when after Stalin's death repressed people were being liberated, was queuing for hours in order to get news of her husband who had been arrested in 1937. She couldn't leave the queue as nobody was allowed back. She had been staying there, tense and worried for so long that blood started to drip from her. While she stood there bleeding, the investigator noticed her and took her into his office. Why do I remember this story? Because to be able to bleed out of worry for a loved one – that is a gift.

There was a time when our extreme poverty was a pan-soviet phenomenon and nobody rebelled against it. I used to travel around the Soviet Union a lot and recall times when having a sausage or pickled herring with bread to eat was a real treat. Our universal poverty became elevated to the level of respectability. Today division has taken its place. One man remains poor while another gets richer. Many talented people are thinking now about how best to use their talent and whether it's possible to sell it profitably.

There are only two ways. Either you do what you consider right putting up with the hard times until the results of your work and your talent are valued and remunerated. Or you agree to do something you don't believe in just for money, and then you have to be prepared to waste your talent. But professions are connected to the attributes of success and put people in some sort of tables. It makes them compete and compare their achievements. When arithmetic's becomes our main concern talent begins to evaporate. Your energy

is integral, you can either take it this way or the other. It is up to us to choose which way to direct our efforts. We have to make a choice. You might later discover that you got your position, made some money but for some reasons the sun is not shining brightly enough. And there were times when you enjoyed the sun and were happy to share this warmth with people.

I went to see a play in a well-known theatre. It was a notable event in the theatrical world. The actors demonstrated their cool, confident skills and there were even some interesting director's solutions. But the most important thing was missing – that nervous tension, that urgency that the actors were giving it their all. The actors were pretending to act; the viewers were pretending to watch. Nobody noticed how stale and vague the performance was. Not long before the end the main actress became suddenly energised, as though possessed by an inner excitement. The audience immediately sensed it. The quality of the contact changed, which is difficult to describe but is always felt indubitably by all.

You might counter: "You advocate tension for your actors, while we on the contrary believe in actors being liberated, just as Stanislavsky taught us". But the liberation which Stanislavsky was trying to achieve so insistently was liberation through tension. Only by trying to achieve the topmost heights can we achieve genuine freedom. The concept of "the torment of creativity" has become old-fashioned and had even disappeared from our vocabulary. Any difficulties or failures during rehearsals are seen as an emergency. It is followed by a crisis of confidence, and actors feel that the director doesn't know what he wants. Everything that isn't achieved quickly is viewed with aversion. But I'm absolutely certain that every instant of true happiness is associated with suffering. Perhaps it's because most of our torments are so superficial that today we have so little real profound happiness.

"How are you going to build up this scene?" - An actor might ask a director almost in the first rehearsal. What an unnatural question! He's not interested in what is happening, he is not thinking about his associations. He takes the bull by the horns: "How are you going to build it?" It is not he who will live through this role, but I who am to

build it. One of the biggest problems with theatre today, is technical acting, "executing" the role. I can name many good actors who in fact are not creative. Many of them are extremely popular, forming a kind of TV national team. But I am repelled by their detachment and coldness. I don't feel their pain, I don't sense their urgency. Some called it untroubled craftsmanship. We might also call it standardised craftsmanship or - depending on the talent – a standardised occupation. In the first case there is at least virtuosity in imitating life, but in the second it is just a hideous dissimulation.

Our poet Alexander Tvardovsky said: "In poetry one can't be a virtuoso." Alas, in our field there are enough "virtuoso-actors " but very little poetry. Moreover, no other occupation frees you from the obligation to think independently to such extent as technical acting. It allows you to 'hide' behind the text that was created by someone else. Among school leavers and students there are generally lots of talented people. Among graduates from the Academy however much less. They are taught to act but not to perceive the world in an artistic way; they are taught to perform but not to create. The profession to some extent insulates us from immediate impressions of life, and human personality is not considered important. This results in the emergence of actors who aren't able to rise above the mundane.

The most dangerous thing is that even school leavers, whom we would expect to be open and naive, very often have the same problem. They see innumerable examples of non-artistic performances and accept that as the norm. Later it becomes very difficult to convince them that Art must be their all-consuming passion, that it is not an occupation but a form of life. This explains the coarseness of acting techniques that we observe. If the body of the actor is their performing instrument very often we see that some tones are completely missing. We have lost the art of experiencing things physically on stage. We've become very inexact and lost the ability to achieve the artistic synthesis of a physical process. We can recall the teaching exercises which showed the truly limitless possibilities of an actor's body. For instance a genuine bruise can appear and then disappear or tears can be shed just by imagining an onion. The actor's whole physical being has to be involved. This is a fundamental prin-

ciple of Stanislavsky: we try to simplify him all the time but life shows how subtle his requirements were.

An actor who doesn't know how to perfect his psycho-physical form and doesn't train every day, like the musician with his scales or the dancer with his bar, will develop an impenetrable layer of armour instead of fragile skin. Every major author dictates their own tune, their own rhythm for the words and movements. That is what Meyerhold meant when he said that a director needs to study music. We can't talk about the polyphony of a performance if an actor can't respond. I have seen the same problem with set design. Actors often play as though there was no set around them or as if it could be replaced by something different. In our profession as in life everything is interrelated. A lack of psycho-physical training prevents the body of the actor from communicating with reality. Not only the skill of expression is lost but also the ability to see and perceive.

Stanislavsky introduced the notion of "emotional memory" which could be trained and developed. Whatever gets in there stays there, but over the years it gradually fades, especially an actor's emotional memory since they have to exploit it all the time. I remember how Eduardo de Filippo was making coffee on stage – just a cup of coffee. That was a true performance. And not only did he act it precisely but there was an additional, higher sense he induced into it - the real joy he felt in doing it. This is Art. For example - what is impressionism? The delight in a sunny day or a rainy one… We on stage can't deliver anything like that, we just deliver words and often not even audibly…

We have become so overprotective of each other, so uncritical. The concept of a "fiasco" has disappeared from theatrical life. We even talk of "failure" rarely. Everything has become blunt and words like "creativity" and "talent" have become nondescript.

In our theatre we try to maintain a certain standard not only through physical exercise but also through psycho-physical training. If an actor stands still on stage with his arms motionless by his sides, it looks like a trivial amateur performance. But we see them standing like this and call it theatre and even engage in serious discussion about this. Our warm-up before a performance is

not just a ritual, although it is that too. It confirms that we maintain a discipline which many drama companies now neglect. I once spent a holiday in the Actors Hall and it was very noticeable - from early morning singers sang, ballet dancers danced and only actors slept, lay on a beach, ate or drank. There was apparently no need for them to exercise since they had nothing to exercise - with the possible exception of their spirit.

Goethe once said that if the stage had the width of a circus rope there would be far fewer people prepared to walk on it. I think it's important to believe you can fall. That's how we know that ovations have little meaning. Whoever walks the tightrope, risk falling down, if not today then tomorrow. Our actors know that tomorrow they will have to walk it again, and walk it beautifully. Once the students in our classes decided to learn to walk the rope. It turned out to be more than a physical exercise – it was a proof how physical freedom can be achieved through tension. We have got accustomed to an actor's carelessness. Stanislavsky used the word 'untidiness'. It is as unpleasant as compulsive tidiness. Stanislavski used to say: "untidy temperament", "untidy feelings", "untidy vibrations of the soul".

We never use terminology in our theatre although we once studied it intently. Instead we talk about life: what is happening with us in our lives and on the stage in these circumstances. Stanislavski tried to hold life within the framework of a rigid terminological system. However he was always dissatisfied with it: scrapping some notions and inventing new ones - and at the end of his life he hardly used them. Whatever is known as a canonical "system" is early Stanislavski.

We want to expel from our consciousness everything that makes our work a technological process. Training is essential of course, but it is not the backbone of our work, it's something alongside the main problems. While we talk about terminology, I think that "school of experience" is not an appropriate term. I think that he meant not "experience" but "living through". This inaccurate choice of term played a nasty trick on the pupils and followers of Stanislavski. They aim to experience something extraordinary whereas they just need to live it. But in order to "live through", great efforts are required including

technical ones. If you are not interested in the form, in its pure dimension but understand that nothing exists outside the form your body must be fantastically trained to attain this level of expression. It should be so attuned that there would be no need to choreograph gestures or moves; an actor who moves well is not the one who performs what has been choreographed for him: absolutely not! The one who moves well is he who lives every second of the role with maximum expression. The arm moves in the right direction of its own accord, the voice and the eyes show it. It is not a question of talent, but of form and training and most of all of research.

My demands of the actors become higher and higher. It seems to me that they lack many skills, since they can't express what they need and sometimes they can't voice what needs to sound. There are so many inarticulate and badly choreographed or plain awkward performances that when we see a bit of live emotion on stage, we are delighted and ready to praise. There is nothing to celebrate because often these "glints of emotion" are weak, frail, and non-professional... The full-bodied, authentic, masterly skills allow you to forget about them, they free you from themselves, they dissolve in the "living through". That is difficult theatre. Directing a performance becomes more and more of a repetitive process, like manufacturing. For an actor it is even more so. The actor does the same thing day after day: he comes to the theatre, rehearses, performs on stage night after night, comes to the theatre, rehearses… Gradually he notices that he isn't rehearsing and creating anything, but just keeps replicating the same thing again and again. So how do we make what we are doing unique?

The everyday course of life always militates against creativity regardless of the vogue or zeitgeist. Theatre, like any artistic effort, is an effort to overcome gravity. It is like swimming against the stream because there was and there will be no stream ever which would take Art forward. The resistance of the material is always present, and in theatre where the actor is creator as well, he needs to overcome his own internal resistance. Just to drag yourself away from the sofa and start using your imagination or doing something in your head, takes an effort, at times a major effort. Sometimes I watch a

production and it seems to me that the actor is not making the slightest effort; he is not even trying to awaken his imagination. That means that the creative process hasn't even started yet. To me the most interesting thing on stage is the actor and his human qualities. It worries me to see them changing under the pressure of circumstances. Because human beings are vulnerable to circumstances. The voice can easily slip down to the level of the mundane. On the one hand I abhor a theatrical voice, on the other I can't stand trivial inflections on stage. Faces and eyes also change imperceptibly. When I notice this I talk to my actors. Maybe sometimes I torture myself and others with my anxieties. I dream all the time of the possibilities of a theatre that we nave not mastered yet. To a lot of people any effort, any work on themselves is only possible with the threat of the stick, under pressure and this seems to them like violence. I sometimes re-evaluate the strength of the people that surround me, perhaps my own strength too. I love our theatre but I am not enraptured with it. It could be better.

All my life I have never ceased being amazed by the people who take the risk of appearing in a new production on stage; who stand up before total strangers every night; who deliver their first words without having the slightest idea how people will react. There is true courage in this and, I would say, even recklessness. Actors play without knowing fear. They are not afraid to stand in front of an audience that doesn't understand a word of their language. They are not upset by the loud voice of the harsh synchronised translation that echoes in the silence of the auditorium. They immerse themselves fully in their roles... In these moments I feel such love for them. And I know that theatre will always live thanks to these actors and their infinite courage.

The director depends on the actor as much as the actor depends on the director, maybe even more. I would not advise anybody to try to tame the actor or to oppress him with authority. It is inhuman, dangerous and unproductive. The acting profession is psychologically very complex; actors can't see themselves from the outside. They are painfully self-conscious, fragile and vulnerable. Critics can't even begin to imagine how hurt an actor can be when

their name is not mentioned or is mentioned for the wrong reason. This is a very serious matter for me because the majority of my actors are also my students and I have been connected to them since their youth. Theatre performance is a product of love in the most biblical sense of the word. If there is not enough love, something is missing from the performance.

I think that all the assumptions that acting is a 'doing' profession and directing is a 'thinking' one stem from ignorance about both professions. That is why in my time I decided to train in both. The director has to be able to do everything that he is asking from the actor. If a cart-wheel is needed – you do a cart-wheel; if it's necessary to sing – you sing. You are the director. A man is capable of much more than he is expected to do. One person does not know that they can sing, another one – that they can be free. Generally theatre is a fantastic professsion. It's a pity that actors don't trust themselves and abandon theatre for the nonsense of show business. Sometime I want to tell them: "Love and respect yourselves because you are doing a good deed, regardless of what people say. Even when you fail you don't add to the evil in the world. But when you succeed, you increase the amount of love in the world a little." We live in a real space and with every day its defiance to theatre grows. We often forget that true freedom in art, as in life, comes through the efforts of the spirit and the will.

One might say, who could be more free than Rostropovich playing his cello? He told me recently how he arrived totally exhausted in some town where he had a recording session planned for a radio broadcast. He was dead tired. Convinced that he wouldn't be capable of recording a note, he still decided to go to the studio: "It's impolite, you know, they've scheduled it…I thought I'd go, pull the bow a couple of times, tell them that it wasn't really working and ask them to reschedule for the next day. But then we began to play and suddenly I felt that with every single note my strength was growing! We recorded for six hours that night!" That is freedom. But the right to play, to use your strength – you have to get it, beg for it from heaven with your relentless work. I tell my actors: "I know that you desperately want everything to go smoothly; in the morning you can

say a prayer, but that won't be enough. You have to also put in the effort, although strain is often in conflict with our human nature".

Do I have the right to put pressure on people, to ask them to make these efforts? I don't know. When I was younger I thought that I had, that I must. An actor doesn't want to work – sack him and that's it. But the older you get, the more you question what is right and what isn't. Today I doubt many things: maybe I must let go a bit; how much one can ask for? These are signs of tiredness. A moment comes when you have to push yourself and, willingly or not, you have to push the others.

Maybe we should praise actors more often, but I've always had this feeling that the moment you are satisfied with something it will vanish, disappear. Theatre is fickle, the fact that something has worked today does not mean it will tomorrow. During rehearsal the actors play just for me and I am the only one that watches them. You always feel doubt: will they sustain the tension tomorrow? Will they hit you like an electric shock the next day on stage? Only with the passing years comes the understanding of how good it can be – the theatre. And how right.

We were in Greece, at Thessalonica where we played Dostoevsky's *The Possessed* in a poorly equipped warehouse. In this new space the intensity of the performance suddenly rose to such heights that I knew immediately in which direction we could take it after the new set of rehearsals. Human relations and connections are endless and boundless. The most interesting thing in theatre is the live texture of human life, which is in fact theatre's main subject. They have used new methods to confirm the authenticity of works of fine art. The results show that the originals exude energy, while the imitations, even the most elaborate ones, don't. How intense the levels of pain, rage, suffering put by the old masters into their works must be, if after hundreds of years they can still be measured? Perhaps it is slightly naive to remind ourselves that the apprentices in Andrei Rublev's workshop had to fast for several days just to start mixing the colours for the great icon painter. Even touching the paints for the future icon with an unclean body and spirit was considered a great sin. Leonardo Da Vinci devised an elaborate system of rituals to educate his

pupils. And in the programme of the studio set up by Meyerhold and Stanislavsky at The Moscow Arts Theatre one of the first lines read: "The theatre is a hermitage. The actor is a heretic."

There is no other creative field that is more prone to fits of vanity than ours. With divine insight Faith has cruelly joined the emotional heights with scheduled of performances; the baring of a soul with constant public exposure. In addition the audience does not necessarily share our pathos and striving. Even in a troupe that is not formed by accident the creative cycles of different people don't always coincide. Often we have to play not what we want, not where we want, and not with the people that we want to. It seems that in our art everything conspires to prevent 'the sleeping beauty from awakening'. When I signed up a new group of students in my class at the Academy I told them: "Together we will study a theatre that doesn't yet and may never exist, a theatre that we won't ever be able to master. We will train ourselves in a dream."

SHORT ETUDE ON *PLATONOV*

Platonov is not on the school curriculum. The play was found only after Chekhov's death without a title page. I read it when Vampilov's *The Duck Hunt* became popular in Soviet theatre. And I was shocked, Chekhov had seen it all hundred year sago. Platonov says a lot of sad things about life. But life is sad because it ends the way it ends and man is somehow drawn to this end.

When the young Chekhov was writing *Platonov* he didn't know that he was ill, he didn't know that he would become a doctor, but he already felt this tragic finality of life. To me this is the most important thing in the play. This is not a play about love, this is not a play about a man who has many women and who is loved by them. There are many plays like that. No, to me this is the book of life: you rush to read it, to understand it, but it closes down not only without answering your questions, but puzzles you with new ones.

Chekhov was the most European of the Russian writers of that time, that is why he drew these shocking pictures of the horrors of Russian life and saw all its menace. He felt deeply the 'slavery' that he himself was brought up into and tried to "thrust the slave out of his soul drop by drop'. He didn't invent this phrase, he was surrounded by that 'slavery', he carried it in himself too and he knew it. We love attributing to ourselves some kind of special 'Russian soul' which makes us incomparable to the rest. Chekhov knew well that this breadth very often came from narrow-mindedness. The Englishman, who, after seeing *Platonov* at the Barbican, said that now he understood why the revolution had happened in Russia, was right. Chekhov pre-sensed this end of an epoch; he understood how the nature of Russian might changes into feebleness and ends in ruins. The vile will of the revolution wouldn't have won without the right reason.

I don't really understand our enthusiasm and oblivious joy as we gear ourselves for the new millennium. We approach it with horrendous results. We ran the whole circle just to find out that nothing had changed. Just our savagery has grown even bigger…

I've always been afraid of all kinds of futurology, predictions and

quick conclusions. All our previous experience has shown that contemporaries are often the least aware of what is happening in their time. And Chekhov is the closest example. *The Play With No Name* was his first dramatic attempt. All his contemporaries were contemptuous. The legend goes that the Arts Theatre leading lady, Ermolova, didn't like it and Chekhov's own brother wrote to him: "You're not meant to be a playwright. Stop wasting your time with this rubbish!" My teacher Zon told us how in the 20's they were in Yalta with other writers and actors visiting Chekhov's sister, Maria Pavlovna. They sat and talked and she told them that she wanted to turn the house into a museum like the museum of Goethe in Weimar. After that sentence, Zon remembered, an awkward silence fell on the room. They felt embarrassed, you see; the sister was obviously very fond of her brother, but, really, how could anyone compare Chekhov to the great Goethe?! And yet by the end of the 20th century, the only truly great writer to come out of the 19th century, the one that stayed with us and went further, was Chekhov and he alone. And it was a century full of heavyweights – Pushkin, Gogol, Dostoevsky, Tolstoy…

The Possessed, MDT, 1991.
Photographer Victor Vasilyev

The Cherry Orchard, MDT, 1994.
Photographer Victor Vasilyev

Brothers and Sisters, MDT, 1985.
Photographer Victor Vasilyev

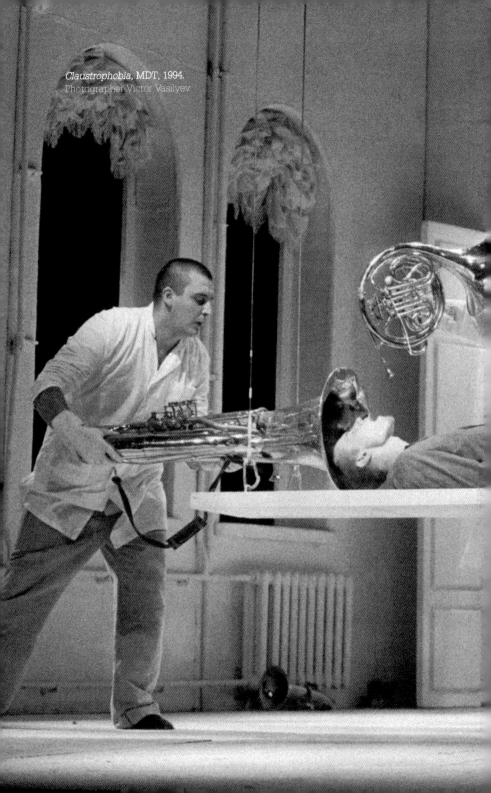

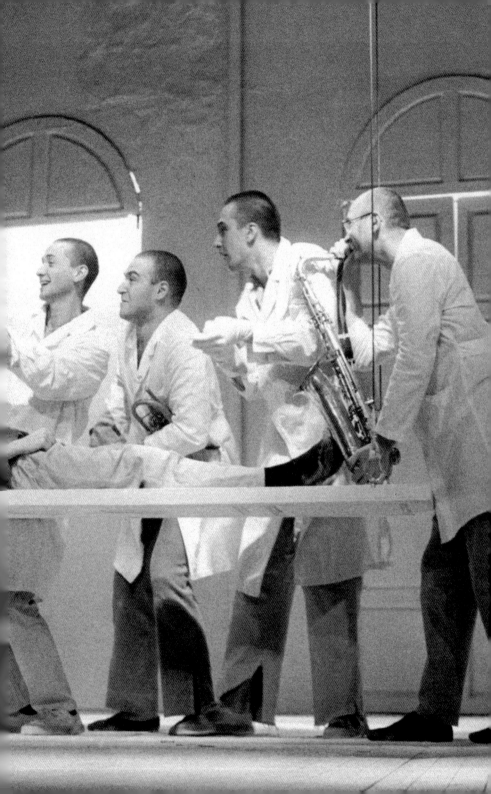

Gaudeamus, MDT, 1990.
Photographer Victor Vasilyev

Lord of the Flies, MDT, 1986.
Photographer Victor Vasilyev

WORKING WITH THE TEXT

Discussion with the participants at the Union
of Theatres of Europe Directors Seminar*

Participant: I have only seen one rehearsal of *Molly Sweeney* but
from what I saw it seems to me that the rehearsals are structured
around the idea that first, as director, you offer a suggestion to the actors and they try to find ways to realise it. Then you withdraw this
idea and propose something totally different. This seems to be a kind
of cyclical process, or to define it better - a spiral movement. I would
like to know more about where this process usually starts?

Lev Dodin: It is very difficult to talk about *Molly Sweeney,* as about
anything that is still a work in progress. You have to put on a confident air and pretend that everything is under control and you definitely know what is what. But the truth is that rehearsals are a continuous quest. On the one hand, the more interesting the work, the
more difficult it is, and vice versa. As for *Molly Sweeney*, everything
here gets much more complicated because we have a very unusual
play (although I think we should approach every play as unusual).
It's a series of monologues throughout and it's very easy to make it
sound like a fiction reading or epic storytelling. So it seemed to me
that it's very important to discover the continuous flow of the inner
life and to understand how the story of one character connects
through some inner motion to the story of another. At first sight the
play is nothing but words but I wanted to explore its inner life, which
is the exact opposite of the words' meaning. We decided to concentrate entirely on what was happening internally.

You are right about the spiral movement of the rehearsals, but I
don't think it was accurate to say that I make suggestions and then
replace them with different ones. I don't replace one with another,
but rather try to develop my previous idea further, make it more pre-

*The International Seminar for theatre directors organised by the Union of Theatres
of Europe, took place in Saint Peterburg, at the Maly Drama Theatre – Theatre of Europe, from 22 January to 10 February 2000. Directors from Great Britain, Italy, France,
Finland, Hungary, Poland and Romania took part. In addition to the workshops, attending run-throughs and rehearsals, the participants had five long sessions of discussions
and analysis with Lev Dodin. These are fragments of the discussions.

cise, make it emotionally more susceptible for the actor. My suggestions change only on the surface, but in essence they unfold as they progress up the spiral that you talked about. If we simply replace some ideas with others, we would move in a circle, not in a spiral. Having said that, I do sometimes make suggestions which are the exact opposite to those we've already tried.

This could happen in moments when the actors have played out the suggested idea, but the result of their performance is so unsatisfying that a major part of the possible truth of that particular situation is left untouched. Then I have to bring something different, maybe even contradictory, into the situation.

If you have seen our production of Abramov's *The House*, you must remember the first scene – the scene where the three brothers meet. They love each other. Mikhail has been both brother and father to Peter and Grigori; he raised them. That's why the scene is full of love, joy and brotherly feelings. During the rehearsals the closeness between the actors grows and I begin to believe in the joy of their meeting. By the way this is not that easy to achieve. Most often on stage you would see the 'good to see you' tap on the shoulder; to escape these cliches is not easy.

It takes a lot of work to get that real feeling, that comes alive on stage. When it happens, the actors are happy and everything seems fine. Then you realise that this feeling is still somewhat flat, lacking the inner contradiction, which creates the tension within. So we go back to dig into the text again. When you read something for the first time, you think that you've grasped everything that is there. But this is a deceptive feeling. In fact, you've only seen the tip of the iceberg.

When you read Fyodor Abramov's novel, you realize, that there is a deep conflict between the brothers linked to their relationship to the sister. The conflict breaks through in full much later, but you are aware of it from the beginning. Mikhail is shaken and excited not just because he's meeting his brothers, but also because he knows that they might have heard about his arguments with their sister. The brothers are glad to see Mikhail but they know about the argument and they just wait for Mikhail to bring it up. Mikhail condemns his sister's behaviour; his brothers however condemn him for this. In

essence, this is a scene of a meeting between antagonists. When you explain this to the actors they look lost: why didn't you say this earlier? If your will is strong enough to persuade the actors, they go back and try again and create a meeting of antagonists. But as always, the cliches come first. Once again it takes time for the actors to go through their own personal experiences, to recollect what and how things had happened to them in order to create a search that's truly alive; that shows that an insuperable barrier stands between these people. Finally something begins to work. Right now they're not brothers at all; they've never loved one another. They're plain enemies! Again it's not right. They must love each other - they haven't met for twenty years. Mikhail was like a father to them and surely they are grateful for what he's done. The actors ask: "Haven't we established that there is an insuperable barrier between them?" We had, but the barrier is between people that love each other. That's where the most difficult part begins.

There is this false assumption that an actor can only play one thing at a time: one emotion, one action; the following moment they can play another. But in real life all the colours are mixed. Only characters in thrillers can just hate each other. In real life, people's conflicts most often grow from their closeness. And usually the stronger the love is, the deeper the conflict. All classical tragedy was based on love. If Elektra didn't love her father, if Clytemnestra didn't love her husband and her daughter so much, we wouldn't have had that whole chain of murders: they were committed in the name of love.

The scene of the brothers' meeting that seemed at first so simple turned out to be extremely complicated. We have to advance on the principle of push and pull: first we remind ourselves about the love and find more and more proofs of it; then we remind ourselves of the animosity and find evidence for that too. There is this concept of the 'second plan', introduced by Nemirovich – Danchenko. It has been wrongly interpreted and as a result, many assume today that the 'second plan' is what one actually thinks, whilst they speak. Like diplomats or thugs: he intends to cut your throat but asks you to to give him a hand. Often actors ask you: "What am I thinking right now?" It's not that easy to answer. Nemirovich – Danchenko said that the

second plan is the character's entire life up to these very words; it is that iceberg, the nine tenths of which are underwater. The question is: where to get the nine tenths from? The director's explanations won't be enough. At this point we have to use life stories, our reflections and imagination and personal experiences. It's very important that the actor's life becomes part of the life of the character.

If we are unable to encourage the actor to juxtapose the character with his own experiences, to recall certain details, then he'll never come alive, he'll never be true on stage.

We were rehearsing Tennessee Williams' *The Rose Tattoo*. The truck driver Alvaro comes into Seraphina's room where everything looks strange and unusual to him. Nikolai Lavrov tried to play astonishment, but it wasn't convincing. We tried to put on some music, to choreograph all the movements, but still it looked very theatrical. Lavrov knew himself that he wasn't getting it right but couldn't understand why. Tired from trying, we decided to sit down and think of some similar moments in our lives when we felt amazement. Suddenly Nikolai Lavrov remembered his first time abroad, when he went to Czechoslovakia, how amazed he was at the hotel where everything was strange and different. So he started doing entirely new things on stage: the surprise was gone, he began curiously examining everything, touching things, testing how they worked. At last Alvaro's behaviour came alive.

Extracting familiar situations and moments from memories, from personal experience, whether psychological or physical, is a very important part of the rehearsal process. Even then a lot depends on the atmosphere at the rehearsals, on the level of closeness between the actors and their willingness to open up to each other and to the director. The problem of a company that has been put together in a hurry is that instead of opening up people tend to protect themselves. The viewer can always see it when actors are closing down from each other. That's why I feel uneasy allowing outsiders into rehearsals. Rehearsal is a deeply intimate process. We have to trust each other.

Rehearsals themselves can become a source of life experiences, which, particularly for young actors is usually limited. During one of

the acting courses we decided to put on Dostoevsky's *The Brothers Karamazov*. The characters of the novel are mostly young people, just slightly older than the actors themselves. We asked the actors to read the novel first and everyone was very enthusiastic: plenty of passion, a lot to play with. As we started probing, it became clear that not only could they not act; they didn't understand any of it either. They had encountered characters with very different personal experiences and different levels of emotional intensity. At that moment we all felt despair -- both tutors and students alike. The students felt extremely depressed and ashamed by their inability to understand characters their own age. But this despair also made them a bit wiser. They knew now what it meant to feel thirst for some unattainable meaning, to seek an answer to a question to no avail. So rehearsals are always a process of gaining experience. Including experiences of how to relate to your partner. If we go back to Abramov's *The House,* the actors who played brothers met and loved each other, then met and hated each other so many times that at some point both feelings had to cross over. Of course for a brilliant actor that would've happened much sooner, maybe even instantly, but such genius is rare.

Today's rehearsal for *Molly Sweeney* is just a small part of a long process when the actor has to solve two very difficult tasks. First of all, he has to reach an understanding about himself and his role in general. Secondly he has to listen and understand his partner, which means to find ways to react to him. I can react to my partner only after understanding who I am. By finding something new about myself, I give my partner a chance to discover something new about himself. This is a ceaseless motion that is very difficult to build and to sustain. Actors by their very nature are deeply egocentric beings, focussed on themselves, preferring to receive than to give love. It's not a coincidence that so few actors are capable of loving on stage - not merely imitating love, but actually loving. Every actor wants to be liked by the audience and they see their fellow actors as more of an obstacle: in all honesty they'd rather have them off the stage, throwing them the lines from the wings. Keeping the actor's egocentric nature in mind, the director has to

persuade his actors that without their partners they won't be able to achieve anything, and so they won't get the audience's love. They can have success only by transposing the centre of attention from themselves onto the other actor.

At the rehearsal of *Molly Sweeney* you saw how the actors tried to find some inner connections between themselves; they began to slow down because they were still very much focussed on themselves and were not able to listen to each other yet. Searching for this connection is very exciting. And you have to be focussed exactly on this all the time: looking, searching, discovering, learning. Because doing something that you already know is quite boring anyway.

As for the beginning of *Molly Sweeney* we didn't start working in our usual way. Usually we read the play and almost immediately we start probing, to use our term. It is important not to lose that feeling of the initial contact with the text. That's why the so-called table period for us continues throughout the entire process of room rehearsals. We try something out then sit back in the circle, we read, we try something else then read again. In this case, making probes without penetrating deeply into the story would've been extremely difficult: the characters here don't act; they tell their stories but never confront each other directly. So just analysing the text itself took much longer than usual. Looking back I don't know whether we made the right choice or not. But that's how we started and just now we are moving towards some probing. What I'm trying to suggest to the actors is that this is a continuous inner narrative; an incessant dialogue with a partner that I can't see or hear, but who exists inside me. It's all difficult and exciting because the outer story does not coincide with the inner one. When the inner story begins to shine through the outer one the tension rises. Still there is a long way to go.

Q: How do the actors' improvisations and the director's ideas co-exist and relate to each other?

Dodin: To me these two concepts are inseparable. Even the best directorial idea will be dead without the actor's life improvisation. During rehearsals we improvise all the time and we constantly adjust and specify these improvisations; and not in terms of what is right but what is wrong. During actors' improvisations I myself improvise

constantly. You begin to compare the impressions you get from these improvisations with the source material. You begin to think what kind of association the improvisations create in your mind and how it compares with what the actors have come up with. You include your own life observations and you gradually begin to understand what is missing in that improvisation, what is accidental about it. During improvisation the actors develop their physical and psychological apparatus. They become more like a finely-tuned musical instrument, or like a well ploughed field ready to absorb the seeds. And your ideas find the right soil and get picked up and developed by the actors.

In *Gaudeamus*, there is a scene at Tatyana's house. Throughout the year we tried at rehearsals different versions of the ending: she'd commit suicide; there would be a collective suicide; she'd be killed. At some point we realised we had come to a dead end: we had many versions but had no idea which to choose. I became desperate and literally instructed the actors how to play the entire scene. Later we added some minor corrections and this episode was included in the production. On the one hand, that was a purely directorial scene, but on the other - it was possible to create it because the actors had tried so many things that it wasn't clear how much of it was my suggestion and how much came from them. And this is very good. I never call our way of rehearsing a 'method', I'm afraid of this word. Like all terms, it's limiting. I prefer talking about a way of 'understanding' or 'tuning' or 'applying one's skill' but never a 'method'. To say, 'We work using this method' would mean we don't work in any other way. In fact we search and are prepared to try everything, until the moment we feel that something's right.

The actor mustn't inhabit somebody else's *mise en scene* or setting or costume. All these should become his own. Even if the costume has been designed expressly by the designer, the actor must feel that he has contributed too. Then that costume will feel like his second skin. Of course, I'm talking about the ideal situation. Very often I invite the actors to the model of the set when it's nearly ready and ask them to imagine how they would like to live in that space: not to play but to live in it. I ask them which spot they like

in particular and what they imagine doing there. Some very interesting ideas come out of this and sometimes the suggestions are very close to what we had thought with the designer before that. It's wonderful when ideas come from the actors. When they put the final set on stage, I ask the actors: "Let's play in this space". There aren't any *mise en scene* yet and initially the actors find it quite difficult to inhabit this new environment. But later they start running and jumping and swimming as happened on the set of *The Play With No Name*. When the one and only *mise en scene* is found, the necessary one, it conjures up all the ones that follow and stems from the ones that precede it.

There is this old Jewish anecdote about a boy, who is getting ready for school. Before leaving he has to have breakfast. He eats some porridge, drinks some milk, then porridge again and milk again. His mother tells him: "You'll be late for school." But the boy says he's hungry. She gives him more porridge and more milk, and then a tiny bun. He's finally full, but he's late for school. His mother is cross with him, and the boy says: "Why didn't you give me the bun earlier?" It's the same with rehearsals. You never know when this little bun will come up. Up to that moment a lot has to be chewed and swallowed. And on top of it one mustn't be late. Sometimes the actors, like this boy, get upset: why didn't I give them the cherished bun, but let them suffer for so long?

In *Gaudeamus* there is a love scene by the piano. In Kaledin's novel there are just a few words, just a hint of romance between Bogdanov and the librarian. The actor and the actress tried to play this scene realistically, flirting gently with each other. But it looked too casual. The next day they tried it differently: the actor threw himself at her, nearly raping her. It was bold, but rather revolting and brutal. And we wanted this scene to be in contrast with all the brutality surrounding the characters. We just assumed that the librarian could play the piano. The actors came up immediately with a new solution: the characters play the piano four hands. The scene had become more interesting but this time it was lacking some boldness or eccentricity. "If only you could've played, not with your hands, but with your feet, that would've been something", I joked, "but of cour-

se it's impossible." Three or four weeks later they showed me the scene, playing the piano with their feet. I am sure that if I had said: "you have a week to play the piano with your feet", they would've insisted that it was impossible...

At the end of Ostrovsky's *It's a Family Affair – We'll Settle It Ourselves* the steward marries the daughter of the master, throws him out of his own house and takes control over the whole estate. When I staged this play in YVT we couldn't find out exactly what Podkhalyuzin and Lipochka would be doing in that last scene. We understood the meaning of what was happening but all our probes didn't feel right: we tried to play it as a celebration, as a triumphant victory; it didn't work. Two weeks later I found myself in Moscow on some business. I remember sitting on a bench drinking brandy and snacking on ice cream, running all the possible versions of this scene through my head. Suddenly, maybe with the help of the brandy, this expression came to me: "They devour their spoils!" I instantly forgot about the brandy and the ice cream, I wanted just to get back to Leningrad to test my idea. The next morning I was terribly nervous: what if I tell my actors about my idea and then it doesn't work? But they were wonderful young actors; they had struggled with me for a long time with this scene and as soon as they heard the phrase 'They devour their spoils', they threw themselves into action. Most of the things they tried had been found and tried before, but this time their actions had a different undertone. When Lipochka and Podkhalyuzin were kissing, they were almost devouring each other: they were to each other also part of the spoils. A lot of new *mise en scene* sprang out of this: when it's devouring you go on and devour. When they were talking about the ceiling, they would jump frenetically to reach it; when a new servant came in, they would ride him ecstatically and so on. Still the solution for this scene was realised thanks to the actors' own improvisations.

It is very important to trust the people that you work with. The actors are used to being directed, to being led all around the stage. But when the actors feel that they've been trusted they can open up and discover possibilities within themselves that even they didn't know were there. If in the process of working the director shows

that he's interested in the actor's opinions, if he doesn't criticise them when they make suggestions, the actors immediately react positively to this.

I staged an opera by Dmitry Shostakovich in Florence, *Lady Macbeth of the Mtsensk District*. We had invited an American singer for the leading part and I wanted to know did she speak any Italian. I asked around. Nobody knew. I turned to an Italian director, who had recently worked with her on another opera. He was very surprised to be asked. 'I've never spoken to her!' he said. I realised that it wasn't the usual practice to discuss the role with the lead singers. The director directs, the singer sings and apart from her vocal performance in the language it was written in, nothing else interests him. As for working with the Chorus, it's even more so. Usually directors give instructions: tenors to the left, baritones to the right. There is this prejudice that that's the only way as it is assumed that Chorus members are the dumbest people of all; that they won't do anything, even if asked, and this attitude of theirs is protected by the unions.

I always try to talk to the Chorus because I can't work any other way. In the rehearsal schedule I had made time for discussions with the Chorus so they asked me: "What's the purpose of this?" I said: "I'll show them the model of the set, tell them what I expect them to do and what it all means." "They won't listen and anyway they won't understand anything", they told me. For a while they did listen just out of politeness; then they began to take an interest, and I have to admit that women tune in much more easily. Gradually a tiny thread of shared understanding developed. Some of them came to me after the rehearsal to say that it was the first time that the purpose of what they were doing had been explained to them. I think that occasion in Paris was one of my biggest achievements; women from the Chorus would even ask questions after rehearsals. They began to think about their role and their presence on stage became much more meaningful. It was enough to introduce some creative element into the rehearsal process in order to see even the most formal tasks accomplished with natural ease.

In this job, you need to be diplomatic, you have to be able to use unexpected tactics if needed. While we were rehearsing the opera a

famous singer approached me and said: "I can't be constantly thinking on stage, it would give me a brain haemorrhage". When I asked him to walk down the stairs in one of the scenes, he told me it wasn't possible because the notes of his part at that moment were ascending. I tried to replace him as you'll never get a decent performance from an actor like that. My request was declined on the grounds that he had a contract with the theatre. So every time he began his antics I would start to snigger, which infected everybody around me and so we would all be sniggering. Next the audience became infected and the manager and the conductor began to wonder why everybody was sniggering in the middle of what was a dramatic scene. Finally the singer was persuaded to take sick leave with half of his payment.

It is important to understand what you can and what you can't accept, and be consistent in this. Actors must see how serious you are about what you want, and believe it. There has to be an understanding that once we've agreed on something, both of us, director and actors, have to stick to it and work to achieve it. And if things aren't working, we have to use all means, all methods to achieve what we want. I'll give you another example from my work on this opera, because in opera things are more formal; deadlines are tight, and to fall behind schedule creates particular problems.

That was my first meeting with the leading lady, a well-known singer, who was offered the main part in my production. I had seen her in another opera and I didn't like her performance. I went to great lengths to explain to her how I understood her role. She seemed to listen, nodded her head, put a word in here and there and it looked as if she understood and agreed with everything. We started the scene and I could see that she was doing everything in the same way as in that performance which I hadn't liked. Her singing was fine but she was truly awful in every other respect. I told her: "You sing remarkably but you're not doing what we've just agreed on." I understand – she said, and again played the scene exactly as before. "Either you don't understand me or you don't agree with me", I said. I could see she was starting to get agitated but managed to control herself and once again repeated the scene as before. When I stopped her again,

she paused for a minute then came up to me and said: "Do you really want me to do what we talked about?" "Yes", I replied - "Otherwise it would all be meaningless." She asked for a break. "How long do you need", I asked her and she said she needed about forty minutes; she needed to think she said. "That's fine" I said. "When you feel ready we'll continue". Everybody broke for coffee while she went outside and sat on the bench. I could see from the window that she was deep in thought. Then she told the assistant director that she was ready, and focussing all her concentration and will, she came back on stage. From that moment we began working as true partners and eventually became friends despite all the rumours about her difficult temperament. She showed that she was capable of changing. To put it simply, she had sung this part for many years and nobody had ever asked her to change anything. Now that she'd tried a different existence on stage, she discovered possibilities that hadn't occurred to her before, and she liked this. Actors in general are convinced that directors don't expect anything new from them and won't demand it in earnest.

Q: How do you start your rehearsals? What is the order - first the text, then the analysis of the situation, or do you first analyse the situation and then go to the text?

Dodin: Nowadays it's different. In earlier years, when I was inexperienced and followed the rules closely, we always started by reading the play and then analysing the story. In his last sessions Stanislavsky used to say that there was no need to read the play: as the story gradually unfolds you'll get to the end. He tried to work in this way on Griboedov's *Too Clever by Half*. He used to say to his students: "You see, I'm not reading the play, I'm guessing what's coming next." Naive as he was, he had forgotten that he'd read and staged this play many times before. And the students would (without his knowledge) read through the play at night... I used to start by reading through the play, then we'd talk and share our impressions. It's important not to let the first impressions fade as you develop new layers and deepen your knowledge of the play. First impressions are the sharpest, liveliest ones. I try to persuade my actors to write them down as even two days later it will be difficult to

remember them. You need a notebook which you can look in and recall your impressions. The next thing, I ask the actors to retell the story of the play. Not to repeat the plot, but to recreate it as a fragment of an authentic life. For example, in Ostrovsky's play *It's a Family Affair – We Will Settle It Ourselves* , which I staged in the YVT, a mature young girl is eager to lose her virginity, but would rather do it the accepted way – by getting married. Her father is too busy making money and doesn't care about his daughter's troubles... The closer and more personal the perspective we take in retelling the story the better, particularly if it's a classic.

It's not that easy, retelling a story. Even though we may have read it many times either together or at home by ourselves – you realise that you've missed so much. When you read you only scratch the surface. Today, when we have the chance to reread Chekhov or Dostoevsky, whose works we've already staged in out theatre, we find so many things that we haven't noticed before. The result and the quality of the rehearsing process is defined by the quantity of details we managed to find. For example: he loved her, then killed her - this story is just a sketch. He loved her, then became jealous, then killed her - this one is a bit longer. He was looking for love; he suffered from being lonely and unappreciated; she was the only one that appreciated him; he fell in love with her; then became jealous and killed her – this time it's much more detailed; many things have been noticed. You can endlessly extend the story in this way. The more details and turns and shades you notice, the richer the process becomes and also the result.

Some directors think that they should invent everything in the story; others feel that they should discover things which are already in the text. With the first approach most often you develop a rational construction or what is called a concept. 'I came up with a brand new concept' you might hear. 'It's never been done before: Romeo doesn't love Juliet, and everybody dies because they are all degenerate swine!' Of course, every concept has a right to exist. But this concept ignores 99 % of Shakespeare's creative material and leaves the life associations completely unexploited. You can limit yourself to what lies on the surface and stage a show about hate destroying

love. But you can plunge into the play's depths and try to understand, how love destroys itself: how it intensifies hate, how it turns on itself...In other words you can go on to discover your own, most painful and real torments in the play.

I was preparing for Richard Strauss' opera *Elektra*. Listening to the music, I noticed that at the most horrifying moments of this story the music reaches the heights of beauty and penetration. I carefully re-read the text and discovered that in the most antagonistic scenes, unexpectedly tender, strange and affectionate words were used. People were having explosive arguments, they wanted to destroy each other, but behind that – a wave of tenderness and affection. When I immersed myself in these ancient stories, I realised that all the clashes between the characters were permeated with love. Love was at the root of the most vicious conflicts there - unacknowledged love, rejected love, betrayed love, humiliated love - which as a result had turned into hatred and abhorrence. This discovery transformed my perception of the story that lies at the base of the opera. It forced me to look at every situation in a different way. Clytemnestra was always thought of as being repulsive, sick, vile and filthy; she was always portrayed as a witch and actresses have always tried to make her look even worse. But examples of unmitigated evil only exist in fairy tales. It's only there that you can have a person who is unequivocally bad. When you study the story, you realise that Clytemnestra herself was at some point humiliated by Agamemnon and the resentment had been growing in her for some time. To escape the loneliness, she had to take a lover, because that was the only thing she could do. But then he didn't satisfy her either as he couldn't compare with Agamemnon. In revenge for all that she destroyed Agamemnon. Now she's torn apart by feelings of guilt; she's looking for comfort from her daughters but her favourite one doesn't show any understanding. The encounter between the two of them is always played like that: "I hate you" – "I hate you even more". But this is not a scene of rows and squabbling; it's complicated, marked by an oscillating scene where two loving people try to reach each other. This is a much more dramatic and captivating interpretation. People are drawn to each other and as a result they repulse each other.

Strauss created for Clytemnestra at that particular moment some wonderfully beautiful music, tender, full of longing and love. This music could only have been composed for a favourite heroine. But this music usually goes unnoticed, because of the cliche, deeply embedded in our subconscious, that Clytemnestra was despicable. And in the background the violin plays softly, softly... Later I read Strauss' letters, and again I discovered amazing things. Clytemnestra wasn't physically sick - she was morally damaged. She wasn't ugly either - she was beautiful. So why then do actresses play her as a freak? In the very first production, conducted by the composer himself, the cliche was already reinforcing the perception, more powerfully than the music.

Another heroine – Chrysothemis, Elektra's younger sister, the one that refuses to hate or take revenge: she wants a normal life, to have a child, to be fulfilled as a woman. One would think it is all very clear: Elektra wants revenge; she has to wait for Orestes to get it; sooner or later he'll come. When I was in Mycenae I stood at the top of that mountain. I could vividly imagine Elektra standing there and waiting constantly, day and night. There are endless plains around, you can see far into the distance. Even if Orestes was to appear a hundred kilometres away she would still spot him immediately. If he doesn't come, she has to think how to do everything by herself. She is intensely concentrated and ready to act. She prepares and waits, in other words she is in a state of action. She stands, waits and thinks... thinks... thinks. If we give her the right circumstances to concentrate and to think, her monologues become extremely interesting. Elektra is one of the two characters that think all the time; the other is Clytemnestra, but she's somewhere, in the palace, we don't see her.

As for Chrysothemis she wants to get on with her life; she rushes around the palace and constantly nudges Elektra: "Wake up! Stop thinking of revenge, let's run away!" She is full of energy, even physically, because she really wants to break free. But Elektra wants to stay. This is the situation, in terms of the chain of events and their inner meaning. But more often people take a completely different view: Elektra wants to act; Chrysothemis however doesn't. So in the

majority of productions it's all staged the other way round: Elektra rushes around the stage as if she's already killed everybody, angry that there's no one left to kill. Eventually she becomes so annoying that you want to kill her yourself. Whereas Chrysothemis, based on the fact that she doesn't want to kill, is considered for some reason almost a negative character and soon begins to look boring. She sits and moans: "Let's just live, don't run everywhere; I want a child, I badly want a baby!" And this wish of hers makes her looks like the lowest and most despicable thing on earth. Instead of a character exploding with energy we get an incredibly tedious being. It is the exact opposite of what is really happening.

People often manifest their inner goals and aims in the wrong way. In Hofmannsthal's libretto just after Orestes kills Clytemnestra, Chrysothemis speaks these lines 'A massacre is taking place in the palace. People are killing each other'. It's true that all this is happening, accompanied by a very loud music and you can't hear the words. If you can't hear the words properly, nobody pays attention to them. In the end, when Chrysothemis finds out that Elektra is dead, when one of her regular fits of love has turned into hatred, she shouts: "Orestes, Orestes!" Hofmannsthal says: "In reply – silence". Why is the reply to this scream to her brother silence? What does it mean? Perhaps we are to assume that everybody's been killed – that Orestes himself is dead and the only person still left alive is the one that didn't want to kill in the first place. Now she is completely alone. There is enough here to stretch the imagination. In the majority of productions I have seen, after Chrysothemis' scream windows get opened wide, Orestes waves happily and ranks of triumphant victors march onto the stage. Instead of silence we get a victory parade. My feeling is, firstly, that nobody has read the text carefully; secondly, people haven't even thought about the ethical meaning of feeling joy after so much murder; thirdly, obviously everybody is more concerned with the opera having a grand finale than anything else. Even Claudio Abbado, one of the most well-read conductors, who has performed this opera many times, every time I start talking about this moment, jumps up outraged: "What silence?" Which is understandable as the music at the end is really loud indeed.

In essence, by talking about *Elektra*, I was telling you about working with the text. This is the part of the process where even we directors can be very superficial. The next stage is working with the actors and if you yourself are not well prepared, you just skim together over the surface of the story. However, if you are thoroughly prepared, if you can imagine the whole story of the play in your head, when you ask the actors to retell it in their own way, you are able to draw the maximum of detail out of them. The important thing is that, as they revise each other's points, ask questions, go back to the text and re-read different bits, they begin to notice more and can suddenly come up with the detail that will define the course of events. This stage of reconstructing the story usually takes several days.

The next step, you go back to the moments where the actors have failed to notice something or have misunderstood its meaning. If you have enough time, and the actors are interested and motivated, you can try to reconstruct the whole story with them again. This time the story will be twice as long, with twice the details and nuances because they've noticed many new things. We start discussing how the old stuff relates to the new, the actors will look deep into the words to find clues about this or that situation.

After that, if you have managed to grasp this sensation of a truly alive, authentic life story, the important thing is to find out where this story began. Where did the story of *It's a Family Affair – We'll Settle It Ourselves* begin? Many would say that it starts with Lipochka's monologue. But I say no. The text begins with that, but not the story. What is the start of the story? Which fact has triggered the course of events that had put the story on this particular track?

It is not easy to find out. Together with the actors you begin to scrutinise different options, gradually getting closer to the event that defined the story.

For example, in Chekhov's *Uncle Vanya* the turning point could've been Serebryakov's retirement. It happened long before the beginning of the play but his retirement changed everybody's lives. It destroyed uncle Vanya's illusions. It brought Elena Andreevna back to the estate, and by doing so it destroyed Sonya's hopes for Astrov's

love, attracted Astrov to Elena Andreevna and finally destroyed Elena's illusions, because, while Serebryakov was working, he was in her eyes much more than an ageing husband. Not to mention that the everyday routine of their lives collapsed: they stopped functioning as before - they stopped taking on time anymore, they stopped cooking porridge. I suspect that everything in the play is related in one way or another to Serebryakov's unfortunate retirement.

Once we've found the initiating circumstance and checked that it's the right one at all levels of the play, the next step, if we want to be consistent in our method, is to find the highest point of the development of the story.

This isn't what they call the 'culmination' in drama theory. The highest point can coincide with the culmination or not. This is the point where resistance to the story's course of events, as defined by the initiating circumstance, is at its highest. The characters can't revoke their circumstances but they try to resist its consequences - they fight it. If you can't regain your husband's love, you try instead to behave with dignity; if you're in danger of losing Astrov, you try every way to win him over; if you can't trust and serve Serebryakov any longer, you try to seduce his wife; if you can't seduce his wife, then you have to kill him. That's how it is for everybody.

Serebryakov's retirement caused the collapse of ideals and illusions for the whole family, and their striving to overcome this collapse leads to a general riot. Everybody riots, even Serebryakov himself. His idea to sell the estate is another attempt to break the chain of events: to go back to the city, to somehow regain his position, to shake off everyone who's hanging around his neck. At some point everything comes together. Sonya, after finding out that Astrov doesn't love her, has to face the cruelty of her father and shouts: "Daddy, you mustn't!"; uncle Vanya sees Astrov and Elena kissing, then the furious Serebryakov grabs his pistol. Everything gets drawn into a knot, a knot of rioting. This moment was preceded by a sleepless night, excessive drinking, declarations of love and a thunder storm as if nature also was gearing up for the riot.

If however we decide that the highest point is uncle Vanya's decision to poison himself, then all the facts line up differently. He was di-

sappointed, he failed in love, he got drunk out of sorrow – it's all turning into a rather boring story about poor old uncle Vanya. It doesn't
always happen arbitrarily: many people think that Chekhov is simply a melancholy writer; they don't look for the initiating circumstances, they just read and stage the text and follow the plot of the story.
But if you look at Chekhov's play as part a of real, personal life story,
and if you correctly identify the main circumstance, you start to feel
the presence of an enormous temperament in Chekhov, nearly as big
as that of Shakespeare.

Let's investigate the story further. It's important to understand
how it ends and what it's all leading up to. It's not easy to do this
either. It seems as if it will end with uncle Vanya wanting to poison
himself. But no, it doesn't. Uncle Vanya sits behind his desk and takes dictation from Sonya; Astrov speculates on the weather in Africa,
then says good bye to Sonya; Marina can't wait to eat her porridge.
But even this is not the end yet. Sonya says something about the sky
sparkling with diamonds. That's what everybody remembers, and
suddenly they turn Chekhov into this great optimist, who believes
that a better life will come and the sky will sparkle with diamonds.
Most of the Sonyas I've seen say these words with pathos. But Sonya
in the play has just gone through a profound shock - she tried to reb-
el, but it came to nothing; she parted with Astrov for ever, she parted from her father; the only person she trusted and befriended has
betrayed her. These words about the sky sparkling with diamonds…
she says them in total despair. Uncle Vanya weeps, because he
knows that after their failed revolt they can't recover their lost life,
they can't get back their lost illusions.

When we have reconstructed the chain of the events, Sonya's
words become clearer. She means, 'we must live, and since we live,
we must endure. We must wait for God to take pity on us and lead
us to a better life - then we'll see the sky sparkling with diamonds,
we'll hear beautiful music and the songs of angels and we'll finally
find rest'. The play ends with a moan of total despair; with a clear realisation that what has happened is irreversible. I think this is a constant theme in Chekhov. It comes up again at the end of *Three Sisters* with the words 'We will live on'. These words are seen as an op-

timistic call to life, regardless of all the facts: the regiment is leaving; Tusenbach is killed; Masha loses her love. But still we must live on. Maybe this is the most frightening of all the things that Chekhov says. He tells us stories of life, full of passion and hope, full of failed illusions and desperate efforts to bring them back, but it turns out that the most terrifying thing is simply to live. This makes Chekhov the tragic poet of the 20th century.

Only after we've understood or felt this deeply can we start our probing: only then can we read through the first scene, try to discover what is the main event there.

(Dodin reads from the beginning of the first act of *Uncle Vanya* and stops at Astrov's line: 'I've changed a lot in that time?")

Marina offers some tea to the doctor. Unwillingly he takes the cup but then hands it back; he doesn't feel like drinking tea. So she asks understandingly: "A drop of vodka perhaps?" This means she knows that he's suffering from a hangover. He says: "No. I don't drink vodka every day. It's too hot anyway". The main point here is the *heat*, the *tension*. This is not small talk about tea or vodka, which is the way you usually see it played out on stage. There are some highly charged points in this first scene that we have to detect. Marina gives him this knowing look: why pretend in front of the woman who knows him so well? She looks at him for a while. This pause is not an empty beat; it's an extension of life. A Chekhovian pause... Astrov notices this look. That's why he asks: "Nanna, how long have we known each other? Have I changed a lot in that time?" She doesn't answer immediately, which hurts him even more: "How long? Oh my Lord, I wish I could remember..." In other words, God knows how many. She's trying to recall them year by year, who died, what happened... It has not been just eleven years; it's been much longer... And judging from Astrov's looks, definitely much longer. She is pitiless, as are all ordinary Russian people: "You were a young man then, you were good-looking. You've aged, my love. Your looks aren't what they used to be. And you enjoy your drink". She returns to where she's started. She confronts him with his alcoholism. That is the source of their conflict: Astrov is an alcoholic, not just a doctor who drinks.

"Yes... In the last ten years I've become a different man. You know why, Nanna? Because I've had to work too hard. <...> Anyway, life is a dull, stupid, dirty business at the best of times. It drags its feet, this life of ours. You're surrounded by cranks and eccentrics... Live with them for a few years and gradually, without noticing it, you start getting a bit odd yourself. It's inevitable. *(Twirling his long moustache.)* Look, I've grown this great moustache. Stupid thing. I've become a bit odd, Nanna... I haven't gone soft in the head yet, thank God; my brains are all there, only my feelings have got somehow blunted. There 's nothing I want, nothing I need, no one I love... except you maybe, because sometimes you tell me the truth and you shake me up a little". I had a nanny like you when I was a child. Marina says: "Do you want something to eat perhaps?"

She is used to this kind of outpouring. She doesn't feel that touched by it now because these confessions don't change anything in Astrov's behaviour. "No. In the third week of Lent I went over to Malitzkoye – they had an epidemic there...Typhus... Peasants lying packed together in their huts... Mud, stench, calves on the floor next to the patients... Baby pigs even... I was on the go all day, not a moment to sit down, nothing to eat or drink... Got home and still no chance to rest because they'd carted over a signalman from the railway. I put him on the table to operate, and he goes and dies on me under the chloroform. And just when I didn't need them, my feelings came to life, and I felt a stab of conscience as if I'd killed him deliberately... I sat down and I closed my eyes so, and I thought: the people who come after us, a hundred, two hundred years from now, the people we're beating a path for – will they ever spare a thought for us? They won't, Nanna, will they!"

That is his way of explaining why he's drinking so much now. But that kind of thing has happened to him many times before. So this is not a noble torment over a lost patient, but rather the traditional Russian justification: the environment sucks you in; patients die; what's the meaning of life; nobody gives a damn...

(Participants and Dodin read the lines in turns.)

Marina People won't, but God will.

Astrov Yes! Thank you. Well said.

This is not at all a benign reconciliation; their quiet confrontation continues because Astrov needs recognition now, in this life and not in the next one. If you say Astrov's line in a tone of reconciliation, the play is over immediately.

Enter VANYA from the house. "

Vanya Yes...*(Pause)* Yes... (Dodin pronounces this with provocation and irritation in his voice)

Astrov Had a good sleep?

Vanya Yes...Very good *(Yawns)*. Even since the professor and his wife arrived, our lives have become chaotic... I've been sleeping at the wrong time, eating fancy lunches and fancy dinners, drinking wine...It's bad for the system, all that! There was never a spare moment before – Sonya and I used to work like Trojans. Now Sonya does it all on her own, while I just sleep, eat, drink... It's not right!

We have a man here who feels guilty that he sleeps. He's in conflict with everybody that would judge him, because he judges himself too. From the moment he lost his illusions, Vanya's whole routine of life has gone to the dogs. In a way what he is saying to Astrov is: "You drink while I sleep". Astrov, on the other hand, is happy to put all the blame on Vanya: "The worst thing is not that I drink; the worst thing is that you sleep too much."

Marina *(shaking her head)*. I don't know! The professor doesn't get up until noon, and the samovar's been on the boil all morning waiting for him. When they weren't here we had dinner at one, same as everyone else. Now that they're here it's at seven. The professor sits up at night reading and writing, and suddenly at two o'clock in the morning the bell goes... What do they want? Tea! Wake up the servants for him, get the samovar out... I don't know!

Astrov And they're going to be here for some time yet, are they?

Vanya *(whistles)* A hundred years. The professor has decided he's going to live here.

Marina Now here we go again! The samovar's been on the table for two hours, and they've gone off for a walk.

(Dodin stresses the words "hundred years", "live here", "gone off for a walk")

In this conversation each one of them comes up with more compla-

ints about the new order in the house. It's like a game. They try to spur each other on.

Serebryakov Splendid, splendid... Wonderful views.

Telegin Quite remarkable, Professor.

Sonya Tomorrow we'll make an expedition to the local forest. Would you like that, Papa?

Vanya Tea, then, everyone! (Dodin pronounces the last words with provocation in his voice.)

Serebryakov My friends, send my tea into the study, be so kind. I have one or two things still to do this afternoon.

Sonya You're sure to enjoy the forest...

This is an interesting moment, this is not just about Serebryakov's ceremonious exit. They are all at odds with him, the conflict is brewing. They greet him with tension; he feels it and tries to avoid it. In this very first scene he avoids the encounter by escaping to his study. It's extremely hard for him to share a room with them and they all feel the same about him. Sonya, to whom the escorting and constant attending to her father's needs has become a real burden, sees Astrov and wants to introduce him. It's really important to her somehow for them to be introduced. That's why she brings up the forest expedition. Her father doesn't respond, so she mentions the forest again as if trying to say: "Look, this is Astrov, he's involved in forestry".

But Serebryakov leaves hastily. Elena has to leave with him feeling extremely uneasy as she didn't even get a chance to say hello to anybody. Sonya also leaves with them, trying to smooth out the situation and keep Astrov happy by smiling on her way out. You can see that so far there isn't a single superfluous word spoken; there isn't a single passive moment. Serebryakov runs to his study, leaving Astrov and Vanya standing there like two idiots. One of them had to resist having a drop of vodka all morning and endure his hangover to avoid looking tipsy when Elena comes; the other had to jump out of bed in a panic that he would miss her return. Marina had to boil the samovar twice. They all hate Serebryakov so much that he has to leave the room. But then when he leaves, it makes them feel like fools - another reason to hate him even more.

The moment the group is gone everybody explodes: see the bastard, what a trophy wife he got for himself!

Telegin's eulogy for Elena is usually played as the pathetic delight of a blissfully dumb Russian man but this is not true. The unhappy but quite shrewd sponger that he is, Telegin can sense that his only refuge is about to explode and somehow he tries to stop this from happening. (Dodin reads Telegin's lines with lamentation and despair). It's as if Telegin is saying: "I'm thankful to my fate for everything, and so should you be. Adapt!" Uncle Vanya can't stop himself talking about her, just like a junkie on crack. She's on Astrov's mind too but he's not really pleased, listening to uncle Vanya's drivelling.

Then Vanya switches to the professor. He is irritated by two things. First, that he served Serbryakov, assuming he was serving one of Russia's geniuses and it turned out that he was serving a nobody. He worked hard, sacrificed himself for him and never got time to fall in love, whilst this nonentity managed to grab the most beautiful woman in Russia. He grabbed her, retired at leisure and now enjoys her in front of Vanya. That's what drives uncle Vanya mad. He's boiling with indignation: "For twenty five years he's been usurping another's rightful place..." He means: my place! There is no philosophy here, Vanya is talking about himself. He is not hiding the fact that he envies Serebryakov either. Astrov openly asks: "Is she faithful to the professor?" Vanya answers with despair: "Regrettably she is."

Q: Do you think Vanya understands that the man sitting just in front of him, Astrov, has also set his sights on Elena and has a much better chance of getting her?

Dodin: Judging by the text, he's so shattered by what he's just realised about his life, he's so blown over by Elena and so inexperienced in love, and he has never met Astrov as a rival, that he's not even up to thinking of that at this moment.

Astrov Why regrettably?

Vanya Because this faithfulness of hers is false through and through. Much rhetoric in it, but little logic. Deceiving an aged husband you can't bear the sight of – that's immoral; but attempting to stifle your youth and vibrant feelings – that's not immoral.

Of course Vanya hopes that Elena will choose him, his feelings,

his youth compared to Serebryakov's. He thinks that she is drawn towards him, but is suppressing her feelings. I saw a production, *Uncle Vanya from 42nd Street,* where uncle Vanya could feed his illusions about Elena because he had every reason to. In that production may be out of boredom or because they were shown to be soul-mates, Elena was so tender and affectionate to Vanya, that it helped me to realise with a shocking clarity that in fact there was nothing between them. This whole relationship with her is a figment of his imagination, just as was Serebryakov's greatness. Although very often we see Elenas with 'mermaid' blood in their veins, walking bored around the stage and evoking not much than boredom in response, this Elena was so alive. Something was stopping her from deceiving her husband, she called it 'mermaid blood' and could never subdue it.

Telegin *(plaintively).* Vanya, I don't like it when you say that kind of thing. Really, now… A man who deceives his wife or a woman who betrays her husband – that's someone who can't be trusted – someone who might betray his country!

Usually this line is played as comical one. But Vanya and Astrov, two mates absorbed in their rage, don't notice how much they have hurt and humiliated Telegin, whose wife has left him. She too was younger than Telegin and, according to Vanya's logic, had done a moral thing. They reduce Telegin almost to tears. "Oh, do shut up, Ilyusha!" – shouts Vanya. He is enraged not just because somebody belies him, but also because being an sensitive person, he knows that he has been mean.

Telegin Let me have my say, Vanya. My wife ran off with her fancy man the day after our wedding because of my pockmarked appearance. < … > I still love her, I'm still faithful to her, I help her in so far as I'm able…

He never knew another woman. This is a strong scene, it immediately puts Telegin into the group of the most important characters, that is on a par with all of them in the main arguments of the play.

Two women come on stage, Sonya and Elena Andreevna, and later Maria Vasilyevna enters. I think that somewhere there is the end of this episode, because the presence of women will make them

change their behaviour, they'll start dissimulating and the situation will change substantially. Serebryakov's appearance, for instance, wouldn't have changed the situation, it would've made it even sharper. But the return of Elena and Sonya abruptly changes the situation. Directors often think in terms of scenes, as all nineteenth century drama is structured like that. But it's better to think in terms of episodes based on events.

Now we have to identify what is the most important event in this episode. What do you think?

Participant: I think, it is Elena's arrival.

Dodin: But she doesn't arrive at this moment. You mean her appearance on stage, for the audience. But you must identify the event from the perspective of the characters in this story, not of the audience.

Participant: Maybe it's the arrival of Astrov because they've been already waiting for him.

Dodin: What difference would Astrov's arrival make? To Elena, to uncle Vanya, to Marina or to Telegin?

Participant: In this scene we get information about all of the characters.

Dodin: But again, this is an outside point of view. Let's imagine that we live in this particular situation. We live, we go crazy, we try to avoid hangovers, we try to wake up on time, we jump on Serebryanikov, we declare our love for his wife. What are we experiencing? Not the characters, but us? Which event? It's not easy to identify.

Participant: For me it's more a matter of what doesn't happen than what does. They started drinking tea, Serbryakov rushed to his office without greeting anybody. The thing that they were all getting ready for didn't happen. For me that is the event.

Dodin: So what were they getting ready for? To lay on a state banquet for Serebryakov?

Participant: They were getting ready to develop some kind of relationship with each other. They were anticipating some kind of game, which did not happen.

Dodin: Now you are fantasising. There's nothing like that there.

Participant: But we can see from the text that they are both interested in Elena. When an old man takes her upstairs...

Dodin: But they lived before and will live after that moment regardless of her. Elena went out with him for a walk in the morning and spent two hours with him, and they were sitting like idiots in that hall. At the end, if Serebryakov had sat down at the table they would have had tea and Elena would have sat down next to Astrov and then something might have changed. But they went straight to the study.

Participant: Maybe the main event is that Elena went into the house with Serebryakov. Uncle Vanya is outraged and infuriated by this.

Dodin: But she goes into the house, into his bedroom every night. You are caught up by one entry and one exit and you see them as events. That's how theatre becomes banal. He came here and we did all these things: "Ah!" He went and we did all these other things: "Oh!" Imagine that the actors are sitting in my reception room, waiting for me to come and start the rehearsal. They wait one hour, two hours, three hours. It's not the first time that they have had to wait, but still I don't come. They get angry and swear, they get hungry, go to the canteen, come back, have some coffee and I still haven't come. Suddenly I show up, I walk through to my office and lock myself in. After that one person might smash a chair, wile another might scream or bang on the door. My appearance will just stir up what is happening already, it will sharpen the situation and bring it to boiling point.

You focus on Vanya's outrage. He's saying this out loud for the first time indeed, but it's not the first time that he's been thinking about it. For three years he's been hammering it into his head that he mustn't put up with this anymore. From the day he found out Serebryakov had acquired a young bride; from the moment he saw her photo; from the moment she arrived at the estate; from the moment she first went to Serebryakov's bedroom and Vanya was left sitting alone all night looking at the closed door. His "why" was born a long time ago. Uncle Vanya has been repeating this word over and over again for the past few days, maybe for the past few months. That's

why he immediately reduces Telegin to tears. It's not the first time that he's done this to him. It hasn't all happened *now*. And Serebryakov hasn't retired *now*. He retired a few months ago and about two months ago he came back with Elena to the estate.

I don't think, it's that simple. It's important to be meticulous, to analyse every possible answer you come up with and discard the wrong ones. At times days and nights can go by, and you still can't find a way to articulate what exactly is happening. You talk to the actors again, you note something or another and thus you move a bit closer to the answer...

I suggest you try to think about what kind of event has happened in the first episode of the play, bearing in mind that the whole story began much earlier.

In our work, the most interesting and important thing is not the answers which are offered to us, but the questions that we ask ourselves. The intensity of our search for answers depends on the quantity of questions we ask.

Lev Dodin rehearsing *Brothers and Sisters, 1986*
Photographer Yuri Belinsky

Lord of the Flies, 1986.
Archive of MDT

Lev Dodin and
Galina Filimonova rehearsing
The House, 1980.
Archive of MDT

HOW DIFFICULT IT IS TO BE A DIRECTOR

About Peter Brook

In the late fifties, as a boy, I went with my parents to Moscow. Maybe by accident or because my 'theatre mania' was already evident, we went to a production of the Royal Shakespeare Company's *Hamlet*. To this day I remember the big-eyed, scraggy young man who, with great simplicity and clarity, was delivering words in a totally incomprehensible language but one that I already knew existed in a Russian version. Only in Russian they seemed more complex so they were meant to be pronounced in a special way. That's how I had heard them pronounced in the Shakespearean productions I had seen so far and in which I'd dreamed of taking part. The simplicity of the English actor initially annoyed me but soon began to draw me in more and more strongly. Looking at this young man dressed in casual dark trousers and a white shirt, looking like me and many other young men around me, I realised something that I hadn't known until then, although I loved reading and thinking things through. He was nothing like the character, nothing like our idea of the Hamlet whom we soviet youngsters dreamed of being. This guy, he was just like me, maybe slightly older, like my big brother. He was embarking on his life, trying to achieve something with that life, and I understood how difficult was the very process of entering on and making your mark in life, how complicated everything in that life was. The things happening on stage were becoming more and more complicated and threatening but everything remained so familiar and recognisable. I remembered the name of that actor – Paul Scofield. I didn't pay any attention to the name of the director: at that time I wanted to be an actor and acting occupied my whole mind. Everything else seemed second rate to me and in the world of theatre in general it was still the era of the Actor...

Later, in Leningrad I saw a production of *King Lear* by the same company. I remember that was the spring of 1964. It was memorable for me not just because of this performance but also because of all the other things that were happening in connection with it: problems in the family; the illness of friends; discussions about Lear with

other students; the ordeal of finding tickets. I was already a student on the directing course at the Academy; I had done some Shakespeare as an actor and I was directing a bit, helping my tutor Boris Vulfovich Zon to stage *Midsummer Night's Dream*. We had also done some workshops on Shakespeare with my colleagues on the course, so as every overconfident young man, I felt almost professional in the field of theatre and Shakespeare alike.

What I first saw during that performance was confusing and even irritating: nothing was what I had expected; at the outset I felt alienated; it seemed to me that the actors were doing things without thinking or just didn't know how it had to be done. But as in Moscow gradually I was drawn more and more into that life on stage. The actors were telling me a very simple story, without haste (though in the play everything was erupting), almost without emotions, although from the start they all seemed gripped by insanity. As a result I was the one that began to get more and more agitated. There was no set on the stage, the way we were used to in Shakespearean production, the way, as we already knew from theatre history books, the greatest achievements in theatre design were accomplished. There were some sheets of foil that were very annoying at the beginning, then I stopped thinking of them and my imagination was freed in such a way that allowed me to suddenly understand the things that I hadn't realised about this play before because I was young and stupid. And there was Paul Scofield again; a bit older, but still very young, who didn't even try to pretend to be an old man. At that time I was fascinated by playing octogenarians, we were all very much into 'transformation' which was very highly regarded. But Scofield, sticking to his real age, was aging in soul right in front of our eyes and this aging moved me deeply because it was somehow related to me: I could age like that going through life's misfortunes, disappointments and unfulfilled dreams... And the English language was so simple, Shakespeare's lines were so amazingly simple: we never learned how to say them in Russian. (Maybe just Smoktunovsky in some scenes of *Hamlet* had reached that light, natural flow of breath.) And these actors - zero pathos, zero declamation - discussing the usual household stuff. Suddenly it became clear that that's all

there is, our usual household stuff, and that decides our fate and the fate of the people around us, and eventually the fate of the world.

Of course, it is only now, after so many years, that I can express my impressions in such an articulate way. But at that time I was just feeling that I was lost; what I saw contradicted all the accepted rules. I remember very clearly how after leaving the theatre I walked for hours along the streets of Leningrad, trying to reconcile my confused thoughts and emotions. My thoughts were really confused and running away from that evening's performance. They were not about theatre, they were about something totally different. This time I did note down the name of the director – Peter Brook - and since then his name began to mean a lot to me.

It was the sixties, the time of the thaw, some news from behind the iron curtain was starting to get through to us. We heard the rumours about the legendary production of *Midsummer Night's Dream* with trapezes and swings. The rumours exaggerated a bit but the theatrical imagination is very prone to exaggeration. And when we were told about the actors swinging above the stage and flying through the doors of the auditorium we gladly believed it: the dream of a theatre that could defy gravity seemed within our reach.

Many years later the Maly Drama Theatre was playing in the same theatre where *Midsummer Night's Dream* had been staged, and I saw that it was impossible to fly from the stage through the doors because they were located on the side. However this detail was obviously unimportant: the belief in the possibility of that flight was stronger than any reality, and that is how the people that had been there saw it in their imagination.

It was a time of reclaiming lost values in our lives. Meyerhold was given back to us, we avidly read about his biomechanics, linked it to the method of physical actions, rediscovered for ourselves Stanislavsky and Nemirovich-Danchenko. What Peter Brook was doing – distant in space but close in time – came to prove that experiments in theatre were not only part of its past. Those things which had occupied the minds of theatre's Greats were still alive, and we could carry on searching just as fiercely and as energetically. All this greatly broadened our idea of theatre, which in the Soviet Union at

that time was full of life, but still had its hierarchies and boundaries firmly marked out...

At the start of the seventies we heard even stranger rumours - that Brook had left the famous Shakespeare company, left behind that brilliant actor he had such an amazing connection with, gathered a troupe of amateurs or very young actors with whom he spent time doing some kind of exercises and on top of that – they had all left for Africa. Soviet ideology had always instructed its artists to go out and study real life; that is why none of us wanted to do it. And here were these people who had left England of their own volition to go to an African village, to study its ways of life and create a performance from that material. Its name – *The Ik* – seemed so beautiful and mysterious.

Then my friend and subsequently long standing collaborator Mikhail Stronin brought Brook's book that had recently been sent to him from England. He translated its title on the spot – *The Empty Space*, and it immediately struck me with its immediacy and absolute precision. It seemed to me that all my life I'd known that the stage was an empty space, I just could never find the exact words for it. I will say it again: contact with Brook makes you discover every time the things that had lived in you mind but couldn't find their expression until then. Precisely 'empty' space, not 'free' as they sometimes translate the title. If it is empty it can and has to be filled, and it can be done any way you want. This emptiness craves, calls to be filled...

Mikhail Stronin translated the book soon after that and for more than two years I never parted with it: I carried it all the time in my bag; read it on my own, to my actors. When something went wrong at rehearsals I would find the appropriate extract for the occasion and begin reading. Did it help? Often not, but I felt better: thanks to Brook I would manage to say something important to my actors, something that I couldn't find my own words to express. Now it is difficult to know how and when certain essential theatrical terms have entered our minds, but I am convinced that to a great extent I owe it to his book. Theatre is first and foremost words and many things depend on the question: do they excite you or not? That the theatre

can be sacred strengthened our old hopes - that theatre may be scant but still hold its artistic values high. This proved that it was worth learning and developing. Brook's words provoked much thought on many different levels: for instance, a small theatre shouldn't be seen as a step to a bigger one; from a regional company you don't have to move to a national one. He was making these little truths sound self-evident and opening our minds to the big and important ones. "Living theatre" – we were saying this before Brook, but thanks to him it had become a defining term that draws a clear and simple line of division: not good or bad; not interesting or boring; not professional or amateur; but living or non-living, that is the most important thing. The non-living kind can have some elements of life, and the living one can have some moments of inertia, but in any case the living quality is the defining one for theatre...

And then, sometime in the 70's, as if by a miracle, I found myself in Paris with a group of young actors and directors. We still thought that it was a total fantasy but our first wish was to visit Brook's theatre. And there we were in front of the Bouffes du Nord with a huge queue waiting outside the theatre.

The theatre itself made the same impression as Brook's productions had done previously: I felt as if I was in the wrong place; either they hadn't finished construction or a refurbishment was still in progress. The building was old and beautiful but the plaster was ruined; seats with no backs; cushions on the floor; a half-demolished stage box; back stage left wide open. Nothing seemed to be ready for the parade of the spectacle as we had imagined it. They played *Measure for Measure*. I didn't know the play very well, I didn't understand much of it, it didn't really touch me but for some reason I was extremely emotional. After the show we met his actors and they were a lot less grand than even the younger actors from our troupe. The French, the English, the Japanese actors immediately started talking about their training and began showing the exercises they were doing with Brook with great delight. Our actors were looking at them in amazement: at home we forget about all exercise the moment we leave the Academy and even in the Academy there are pro forma in the programme. These actors after a

hard performance for more than an hour continued to show us with pleasure how they trained...

Later that night I realised that the place we had just left was in fact the true embodiment of living theatre. Everything, starting with the building, was set to free us from the familiar and the mundane and transpose our perceptions into a different dimension. Even if you don't feel close to the performance, you still feel that excitement. To us, who had been used to judge everything in theatre by the yardstick of success, which means in market terms, regardless of all the talk of aesthetic and moral values, Brook's theatre was proof of the superiority of other, highest values. It was a testimony to the assertion that true theatre is like a house full of living spirit, a house for whose inhabitants the performance is part of life itself and not a purpose of existence.

Later I saw in the Bouffes du Nord an extremely interesting production on *Ubu* and the divine opera *Carmen*. After reading Stanislavsky and Meyerhold on opera, I wanted very much to believe that opera really was a living, exciting art form. But everything that I had seen so far defied all their convictions. It was true not just for the opera. The reality of theatre very often is miles away from the theories of the classics and because we live in reality we are inclined to trust reality and not the classics. But Stanislavsky and Meyerhold knew what they were talking about, including opera. Brook's *Carmen* was proving it. Singing was as natural as breathing to the actors and they moved in the same way as they sang. Gradually you forgot that this was a vocal art form because such an absorbing musical and dramatic story was unfolding. Every time I stage an opera I remember this astonishing performance. Opera professionals were not unanimous about it because it 'did not fit the mould'... That is, by the way one of the possible definitions of what Brook was doing.

And then the unimaginable happened - Brook came to see our *Gaudeamus* in Paris and so we met. It was so unexpectedly simple and easy. It was not a meeting with the famous Master but with a man that you feel close to and who feels close to you because of what we do. A friendship, I dare say, was born, a friendship I never dreamt

of and that by becoming a part of my life will always be a most wonderful gift from destiny to me…

Brook's new productions move further and further away not just from general theatre but also from his own work of yesterday. I saw his *Cherry Orchard* three times: in New York, Moscow and Saint Petersburg. On each occasion I experienced the same amazement and the astonishing liberation because there was nothing on stage to remind you of a usual Chekhov production, but it was a true incarnation of 'the life of the human spirit'. As students we had made so many jokes about this term of Stanislavsky that had nearly lost its meaning, but it is the best description of Brook's work. The form of the performance was almost invisible. Brook was less and less concerned with the form. Instead something more ephemeral was coming to life; it pulsated through the existence of these people on stage, who looked nothing like actors. The less they looked like actors the stronger you felt that beat of inner life. I don't think that in Russia *The Cherry Orchard* was given the appreciation it deserved, maybe it was misunderstood. People expect great shocks from great directors. Not catharsis – the soul is never ready for that – but exactly a shock. And here there was an absolute and sublime simplicity which in essence is the greatest heresy of all. This simplicity always stunned me in all of Brook's productions. Since the time of that first *Hamlet* just its measure has grown and it has been elevated to an exceptional, almost improbable level of subtlety. In some instances you feel something that is almost a pure emanation of spirit.

One of my last impressions of Brook's work was *The Man Who*. When a year earlier Peter had told me that it was about mental patients my imagination drew images of something dark and piercing, not unlike his much earlier blazing production *Marat-Sade*. But what I saw was the life of the mind drawn with the lightest touch, with the finest brush, shown almost without compassion or concern for the audience's reaction. Very recently a friend of mine was severely damaged by mental illness. By communicating with him I suddenly realised the stunning accuracy and humanity of Brook's production. Thanks to his enormous talent and to the astonishing calm of spirit he possesses, he had succeeded in seeing the

psychological state of the patient from within; where you are not aware of the tragedy of madness, because your madness is your sanity and your confusion is your logic. Brook had again shown us what in truth is happening within a human being.

I have to say that the inertia of perception is a fantastically strong thing. We refuse to believe that many things in the world are not happening the way we perceive them. Brook's power – although this word doesn't go well with Peter's delicate, calm, almost translucent personality – lies in the fact that for more than fifty years he has continued to destroy all existing stereotypes, one after the other, starting with himself, his own views of man, the world, the theatre. And he continues to ask the same questions again and again. It is not by accident that one of his shows is called *Who's There?* Who is there in the theatre, who is there on the stage? who is there in the play, who is there in this life? This constantly occupies his mind. His life, as the life of Stanislavsky or Meyerhold, is an incessant process of asking questions, to himself and to us; questions that don't have final answers because from each answer springs a new question. It comes to my mind that a life like that requires ferocity, but the word is so unlike Brook who is absolutely free and natural in all his expressions and who simply cannot live in any other way.

Remembering Giorgio Strehler

The fifties were ending, the sixties were beginning... The iron curtain had not come down yet. There was a long way to go, but it had been pulled back a bit. Peter Brook and Jean Vilar had come to the Soviet Union, and their names sounded like music to our ears. We were young and in love with theatre and among the foreign names there was one that was particularly melodious: Strehler. Some had seen something, others heard something, but no one could say coherently what it was all about. Then an article on Strehler's snow white *Cherry Orchard* came out, and it seemed so far away from the naturalistic Chekhov that was prescribed in soviet theatre. Then came the book where remarkable, sincere, poetic writing was placed next to pages of serious and, in our view, boring social analysis. We were overfed with analysis, we couldn't understand what it had to do with living theatre.

Finally Piccolo Teatro came to Russia and we saw *Campiello* – a tale full of magical talent and truth, a combination of a kind of brand new realism and symbolism. There was a lot of snow on stage but, not believing that they could have that much snow in Venice, we thought this was Strehler's genius of invention at work. I was already teaching at the Theatre Academy and I went and stole some snow from the stage with my students. Years later, when we played *Gaudeamus* in Budapest at the festival of the Theatres of Europe, there was a reception after the show and Strehler, who had seen it, came across the big hall straight up to me and said in front of everybody: "That snow is mine! I did it first, I had the first snow!" "Of course, of course you were the first, Giorgio, I told him, because by then we already knew each other – "We even made the snow look like yours." His expression changed and he said to me: "No, no it's a different snow. Everything is different, but I'm glad that you remembered *Campiello*."

Then The Assembly of the Union of the Theatres of Europe took place but I sat only through a couple of sessions because I hate all meetings and assemblies. I was surprised, even stunned to find that they consisted of Giorgio's extended monologues. He could go on for

hours without stopping, even when other speakers had taken the floor. They couldn't translate it all and I didn't understand a lot, but these monologues didn't just make us smile: there was this strong, sweeping, at times inarticulate, passion breaking through. Now that there is no one to give us eight hours of monologues, the Assembly seems boring without him. We began to understand what he wanted to say, what his soul shouted about, breaking up the order and turning the Assembly into another lyrical, comical, tragic act.

Then there was the premiere of our *Brothers and Sisters* in Milan. Contrary to habit Strehler sat through the whole performance, although a couple of times he got so agitated that he had to run out and come back in again. He was sitting in the last row and thought that nobody could see him. But I watched him as I wanted to observe his reactions. At the end he threw himself on me, started to kiss me and said repeatedly: "My brother, my brother!...Fratello, fratello!" He was crying, I was crying too. It's a private moment. Maybe it's not right to talk about it, but when I learned that Strehler had gone, this is the first memory that came to my mind.

Of course after that I immediately remembered another occasion. After the premiere of *Brothers and Sisters* there was a banquet in a beautiful palace close the Milan Cathedral. We talked a lot, he hugged and kissed our actors and we made plans for him to come to do some work in our theatre. I was suggesting Goldoni, he was saying Mayakovsky. His imagination was running riot but I didn't interrupt because it was interesting to listen to him. Then somebody dragged him away and I saw him getting ready to leave. The party was still in full swing, the young people were having fun, singing and drinking, and - just for a second - he looked so tired and old on his way to the door. Suddenly my wife and I felt this sense of horror, as though he was going out of our lives for ever. We ran after him across the big hall, stopped him and talked some more, then had to say goodbye again. When he finally left that same dreadful feeling of loss came back to us.

Happily, that was only a premonition of the very distant future. We met and talked many more times, we admired the Strasbourg cathedral together, we made plans for our two theatres to work together.

I signed some petition against something that had made him angry; I wasn't sure what it was, but I knew that if it made him so angry I had to be on his side...

Christmas was just round the corner. He sent us a card, I sent him ours, and with Christmas came the sad news that he was gone. After only twelve rehearsals of *Cosi fan tutte*. A friend of mine told me that the production had a long run and full houses, which was unusual for an opera in Milan. It made me think again how lonely he was. This feeling would often haunt me because I saw reflected in his loneliness my own, the loneliness that could take hold of me and had already done so at times, although you don't want to admit it or accept it.

The loneliness of the artist, of the director, has accompanied me since my youth. I remember when I was still a student, one of my teachers had staged a new production at the theatre. After the show we waited at the stage door to congratulate him. The actors came out, then he came, alone. Alone! After his premiere! It shook me so deeply, I still remember the horror that seized me. I had thought that all his actors would be with him; after all they'd worked together, he had created their parts. But he was alone, so glad and surprised to see us there.

Giorgio's loneliness was erupting in his lengthy monologues, exploding in his sophisticated productions, driving his social campaigns. One of the last Mohicans of the post-war generation, he was constantly trying to unite us. This idea of artists and people united made him, who was considered a great egocentric, one of the most sociable, generous and large personalities I've known. Strehler lived with his ideals, illusions and hopes. Many of his ideals vanished with the passing of the century, many of his illusions were blown away. Pray God that his hopes are not taken away from us too. Theatre, when it is art, lives only through its despondent hope, through its great illusion that loneliness can be overcome.

Innokenti Smoktunovsky

Smoktunovsky was a great actor. I think that his talent never developed to its full potential because that kind of universal talent, of almost Renaissance proportions, was practically impossible to realise in the frame of Soviet art. Of course some exceptionally brilliant pieces did come to life. There was prince Mishkin in Georgiy Tovstonogov's productions based on Dostoevsky's *Idiot*.

There was Iudushka Golovlev in my staging of Saltikov-Shchedrin's *The Golovlev Family*: the process of working on this production was painful, creating even the smallest things was painful; the characters in the play were dying one by one, in the same way that the regime of power in Russia was dying too. Then there was Hamlet; not all of it, but some episodes in Grigori Kozintsev's film, even though it is an enormously talented film. I think that Smoktunovsky was one of the best Hamlets of the twentieth century.

And of course there was Detochkin in Eldar Ryasanov's *Beware of the Automobile*. In this role he used the Don Quixote and Mishkin's tones from his palette. There were some other roles in theatre and film. But on the whole Smoktunovsky's talent was not fully exploited. The usual Soviet repertoire of plays fitted him like a child's shoe on an adult foot.

He was incredibly gentle and honest, and sometimes this made him appear strange to people who didn't know him. He did not fit at all within the official system. His could not overcome his eccentricity and never really tried to do so. I think this was his way of allowing his inner freedom to find expression. Some people thought he was pretentious while others thought that he was showing off. But he was simply expressing himself. They also used to say he had a difficult character, was fastidious about his work or would only show up at rehearsals when it suited him. The truth is I never experienced any of this. My relationship with him was a continuously happy one. It started from the very first moment I went to the Arts Theatre in Moscow to direct *The Old Man,* based on Yuri Trifonov's renowned novel where Smoktunovsky was invited to play the lead. When we first talked on the phone, he said:

"Thank you for thinking of me, but I'm not sure I will... I won't manage.. I don't think I'm capable of playing this character".

I thought to myself: Talk about capricious actors! It's such a magnificent role! What more does he want?

Then we met again, began to talk and Smoktunovsky exclaimed: "Don't you understand? He was a bolshevik - how can I play him? He killed, destroyed people's lives...

I tried to persuade him in every way I could:

"But surely you can see that he's trying to make sense of all this, he's close to repentance".

"They never repent - they can't repent! This is absolutely impossible!"

I remember that even to me (and I had already had some confrontations and personal clashes with officials and thought of myself as a man of conviction) Smoktunovsky's position seemed too harsh and implacable. Only later did I realise that as early as the late 70's and early 80's this man had very strong opinions and was not afraid to express them. Naturally, he was not a dissident, he didn't voice his views in public, but they were his guiding force.

Eventually, he agreed to play the role. He liked the dramatisation of the novel, he understood a lot about the character. I am convinced that he would have played it brilliantly, but the production was banned and was never allowed to enter the theatre's repertoire.

We met again while working on the role of Iudushka Golovlev. He liked this role. He had a great feeling for the classics, he completely identified with them, they fitted him like a glove. And the way he worked - I would say he worked like a junior student. He used to write down every word, not because what I was saying was that clever but because he needed material for his work. He used to sit and write all the time. There was a crowd of young actors sitting around him with crossed legs. They never wrote anything down, nor remembered a word. But he sat and wrote. His play text was covered with his notes. Later, during the run of the play, I would go into his dressing room and find him sitting and re-reading these pages. Before every performance he would immerse himself in the role again. And even after a very long break in the repertoire he

would come back to the character without losing anything.

We had to rehearse over a long period of time because of difficulties with the set. They were beautifully designed by the very talented Eduard Kochergin, but the technicians were constantly saying that they were impossible to realise. We spent almost a year rehearsing on stage, but they still couldn't sort out how to make the set work. This became a torture. But everyday, I would come in at 11 o'clock in the morning and shout: "Innokenti Mikhailovich!". And from behind the closed curtains Smoktunovsky would sneak out in full costume nodding to me reassuringly: "I'm here, Lev Abramovich!"

Only then would all the other actors start coming out – less great, less famous, some of them very young, dressed in jeans, boots, fur coats. Some would throw their coats on the floor, some would come up on stage in boots, some we had to send back to change...

He would never blame anybody. He would never make anybody feel uncomfortable or embarrassed from being next to such great actor. This always amazed me. Oleg Borisov, for instance, could at times be very harsh with a colleague, of course because of some artistic or ethical argument. Smoktunovsky would defend his artistic point of view using just his own craftsmanship, it was all very organic; he never tried to prove anything. I have never in my life, either as director or as spectator, seen a more organic actor. But he had an organic way of existence.

He took me once to his flat to show off his new furniture. There were two sets of kitchen units which he had finally managed to buy on his 'massive' earnings, and he was one of the greatest actors of the 20th century! He had fitted the whole flat with these kitchen units because that was the only furniture he could find. But he was sincerely pleased with the result and never complained or blamed anybody.

He was an introvert and very private, but sometimes he would open up. Once he spent almost two days in our flat, with me and my wife. He was having some kind of crisis and he just dropped by. He had a parcel he clutched to his chest. It was the 1st of May and state establishments, including theatres, were giving away small

packs of treats for the occasion. "Can I come in?" he asked. "I'd like to stay with you for a while." And he handed over a bottle of vodka and a tin of caviar, the gift the state had designated for actors of 'national' status.

He had a coat and hat on, and slippers. We ran to the shop, bought some quick-fix stuff and sat around the table for hours. He talked about his childhood, about the war when he was taken prisoner, and his smart ideas in the camp, which were all very naive, and about his bravery - the sort you don't express with your fists.

His soul was an amazing barometer of human relationships and the spirit of the time. I think he departed from this life not only because he was ill and tired, but because everything around him was becoming too cruel and harsh to bear... This cruelty crushed his delicacy and gentleness; it pushed and pushed until it finally crushed him.

Oleg Dmitriev as Sergei Voynitzev

The Play With No Name (*Platonov*), MDT, 1997.
The last rehearsal before the opening night.
Photographer Victor Vasilyev

Tatyana Shestakova as Anna Petrovna
Oleg Dmitriev as Sergei Voynitzev
Sergey Kuryishev as Platonov
Maria Nikiforova as Sasha Ivanovna

PLATONOV Observed:
Rehearsal Notes

Sergey Kuryishev as Platonov

The Making of *Platonov*
by Anna Ogibina

In 1977 Lev Dodin wrote his own dramatisation of *Platonov* and submitted it to one of the Moscow theatres. On the title page it reads "A. Chekhov. *The Play With No Name* in four acts (*Platonov*)." The staging was not realised on this occasion, but in 1991 Dodin came back to his long-standing idea and restarted work on the play with his students from the Saint Petersburg Theatre Academy.

Initially they were just studies of extracts from Chekhov's various works, then etudes on *Platonov* itself. Later Dodin started to involve graduates from his previous acting class of 1984-89, who had already done *Gaudeamus* (premiered 11 July 1990) with his current students and had later cooperated on *Claustrophobia* (premiered 18 February 1994). They worked on the etudes during the tour of *Gaudeamus* in Paris (March 1991).

In August 1995, after work on the etudes had continued for more than five years, Dodin did a provisional casting and started the process of reading and analysing the play itself. During the 1995/1996 season he brought in other actors from the Maly, while the designer Alexey Poray-Koshits worked on the set. In January 1996 Dodin showed a model of the set to the actors and talked to them about his idea of having jazz and live improvisations in the music score.

In the summer of 1996 regular rehearsals began in the studio room at the Academy, and the actress Tatyana Shestakova joined the cast. There was a period of 'probing' during which each of the actors could try out different roles on their own initiative or at Dodin's suggestion. Next the cast moved to probes of extracts, scenes, acts, and then the whole play.

In August the first rehearsals with a real set took place. The auditorium and the stage were revamped entirely. The stalls became a sharply rising amphitheatre, the first two rows were taken away, leaving only 260 seats instead of the usual 400. The 'sandy bank' surrounding the 'pond' literally started at the audience's feet, going over the orchestra pit, the water tank being placed in the stage's hold. Steps led from the 'banks' to the exits, small bridges crossed

the water, everything around the pond was built in solid wood. Behind the wooden back wall of the 'bathing place' with its gate opening, taking up the entire back stage, was the gallery where the orchestra was placed with the grand piano and percussion. Dodin cast Sergey Kuryishev in the lead and then did a few runs through still changing the actors in the other parts. There were no fixed mise en scene, the action flowed freely taking up the whole available space.

In the new season between 11 October 1996 and 1 March 1997 Dodin went back to room rehearsals. By then some cuts in the text had been made and the action now started with Platonov's arrival at the Voynitzev's estate. The casting was by then more or less fixed. Rehearsals took place in a circle in the rehearsing room. Actors would read their parts sitting on the chairs, then stand up, move around or approach their partner engaging them in their part. Dodin would still ask this or that actor to try a different part. That was the time when the stage version of the play was finalised: monologues and scenes were cut or re-ordered, some lines from Chekhov's drafts were introduced and the title was chosen – *The Play With No Name*.

Work on the music was continuing; Dodin shared a memory from his childhood of a melody 'The Cherry Branch' and Kuryshev learned to play it on the tuba. Sergey Kozyirev took violin lessons, and all the ladies piano lessons, from tutors at the Conservatoire. This was an enormous task; the musical numbers grew to one hundred, but in the show only twenty five were eventually performed including: Bonjour Paris, Le Chaland Qui Passe, Riverside, Hunters' March, Youth and Virgin, Wedding March, Nocturne (Chopin). Andante (Vivaldi), and fragments from Mahler's 5th Symphony.

By the end of that year Dodin came up with the suggestion of bringing onto the stage what originally had been happening offstage – the lunch party. A table was laid out in the middle of the circle, actors sat around, talking, arguing, sorting out their relationships: there was a full-blown life going on uninterrupted at that table. Now and then some of the actors would get up from the table and come downstage to play a scene, then they would go back

to the table to continue their lunch. Two parallel texts were devised – one for the table, the other away from it. For the table conversations the first four scenes, some cut monologues and dialogues and Chekov's drafts were used. Four versions of this text were devised and tried out. Everyday objects started appearing in rehearsals: the table settings, a bench, balloons. In the show the lunch takes place before the spectators' eyes. After the scene between Platonov and Osip the table is taken downstage, laid out and chairs are brought too. The characters sit around the table, eat, then leave, sing, dance, play music, observe others, go back to the table. The life on stage acquired texture and depth and Chekhov's text was still there in full.

On April 23 rehearsals were moved to the main stage. By then yet more cuts had been made. Rehearsals continued on the stage of the Maly until on June 24 the company left for Weimar, where the production was staged at the Weimar festival with its director Bernd Kaufman. At one of the dress rehearsals Dodin proposed to perform the play without the character of Triletsky, so some of his lines were given to Platonov. The last but one dress rehearsal was performed with Triletsky restored, but Dodin finally settled on the version without this character, thus a major re-editing of the play took place. The premiere was on July 4th in Weimar.

In September 1997 just before the Saint Petersburg premiere a few runs through took place. Dodin had made some additional edits - shortened the third and changed the fourth act using his dramatisation from 1977. During those rehearsals Dodin changed the ending of the performance too. In Weimar there was music, everybody was dancing on the bridges across the water, then rain started falling on their heads. The actors were pressing themselves against the walls trying to hide from the rain; Platonov was lying in the hammock on the water. At the Saint Petersburg premiere all the characters, apart from Platonov, after Bugrov's line 'Peace to the dead', lift their glasses, sit quietly by the table sipping cognac and remembering Platonov. The music from the beginning of the show plays, rain starts falling on Platonov cutting him off from the rest of the crowd, darkness slowly falls, a ray of light just for an instant

playing on Platonov's body spread on the water. Lights come up, everybody is frozen in their places, but Platonov is not there, neither is the hammock, just the dark water is flickering under the lights. Lights go down again, then up again and the stage is empty, there is nobody left. The music ends on the highest note.

The rehearsal notes of Platonov are in two parts. The first part covers the analysis and reading of the play that started in August 1996; the second part includes the rehearsals that took place at the studio room of the Academy and the rehearsal room at the Maly in August 1996. The notes end on March 1st 1997 when the production moved to the stage.

This is an attempt to present the rehearsal process as a narrative. As a result a kind of dramaturgy is created – there are conflicts and plots and characters: the director, his actors and Chekhov himself.

Anna Ogibina has been Lev Dodin's long-standing assistant since 1988. The transcript of the rehearsals of The Play With No Name (Platonov) consists of more than 500 pages and covers two rehearsing periods in 1995 and 1996. We have chosen to publish a substantial par of the first period - the analysis and reading of the play, up to the end of Act One.

From the publishers

REHEARSAL NOTES

Day One

Dodin: Let's try to understand what exactly Chekhov had in mind in this, his first play. Let's see… **Anna Petrovna**, young widow of General Voynitzev; **Sergei Voynitzev**, son by General Voynitzev's first wife; **Sofya Yegorovna**, wife to Sergei; **Porfiri Glagolyev**, neighbour, landowner; **Kiril Glagolyev**, his son; **Gerasim Petrin**, wealthy merchant; **Pavel Shcherbuk**, a Kalmyk, neighbour, landowner; **Maria Grekova**, chemistry student, twenty; **Colonel Ivan Triletsky**; **Nikolai Triletsky**, doctor, son of Colonel Ivan Triletsky; **Abraham Vengerovich**, Jewish businessman; **Isaac Vengerovich**, Abraham's son, a student; **Timofei Bugrov**, merchant; **Mikhail Vasilievich Platonov**, schoolteacher, twenty seven…

It's very interesting that Platonov is mentioned only after all these other characters, only his wife is listed after him and last of all Osip, the horse-thief… One could say that it is the order of their appearance but still it looks a bit demeaning… **Sasha Ivanovna**, wife of Platonov, daughter of Colonel Ivan Triletsky; **Osip**, gypsy horse-thief, and then there are the servants and so on…

We must learn to interpret the details, to pinpoint the emphasis, to highlight the important remarks, the pauses, the dots; to find ways somehow to fill in the spaces in the text. Of course, gradually we'll get good at this. But the most important thing for the present is to grasp the essence of this Chekhovian story and to understand exactly what happens in it. (Reads the remark) *Anna Petrovna is sitting at the piano on the veranda, her head bent over the keys, Nikolai comes out of the house.*

Act One
One

Nikolai Not playing?
Anna I'm too bored to play.
Nikolai Well then, let's have a cigarette, *mon ange.*

Dodin: There is this excitement and tremendous energy about Triletsky. He has been up and about since early morning and he is wrenched by intense feelings for Anna Petrovna. Later he won't be able to keep it to himself and he will erupt: (assumes Triletsky's role) "There is something about her. Even to a man like me. She's unsettling… Anna Petrovna turns me down and still I love her… She's the only woman alive who could reconcile me to platonic love." (Act Two, Scene One, One). It means that we have here a case of platonic love. A very strong one. We have to bear in mind that this isn't their first meeting; it all started at least six months earlier. Triletsky had come rushing in here very early in the day (we don't know whether it was by himself or with his father) and gone straight to the veranda where Anna was standing. He says that he's hungry, that he has come for the pies, but perhaps he went for the pie just to justify his rushing onto the veranda? Obviously he's quite aware of her situation. After all that's all everybody's been talking about and the announcement has already been published in the newspaper. By the end of this scene Platonov will mention it. The announcement that Anna Petrovna's estate has been put up for sale is an event of major importance. It would be as if you had just heard that the Maly Drama Theatre had been rented out to strangers. This means that everybody knows what's happening and they are all talking about it. Triletsky seizes the moment, he has caught her by surprise while she's alone and in a state of complete despair. He has this strong impulse, this urge to give her some kind of support. It's a different matter how he manages to put this across, what it looks like from outside and whether he really is a decent fellow. These are all different questions. However he throws himself into it with all his heart and soul. What would Triletsky have wanted from her exactly? He can't offer her his hand and heart; he can't truly believe that she'd marry him even though he's a bachelor…It's more likely 'what the hell, there is no money in this, but money's not everything'… The immediate thing he's hoping for is that she might sink her head on his chest and start crying so that he can comfort her. It would have been so nice! For Triletsky everything starts from a very strong, ingenuous impulse - a belief that people will respond to him - but often this attitude provo-

kes exactly the opposite reaction. (To the actor) It looks as if Anna Petrovna is just answering your suggestion to have a cigarette but somehow the exchange turns into a confrontation... (Assumes Anna's role): "Take the lot, if it means you'll stop pestering me." I think she's been trained to hide her feelings, but how successful she is remains to be seen. Later Triletsky will say: "Will somebody tell me what's happening to the General's widow? What's going on?" (Act Two, Scene One, One). There are obviously things that can't be covered up entirely. In fact, as with everybody, Anna Petrovna is not that successful at hiding anything, although we all like to delude ourselves that we've managed to preserve our secrets... Shall we try this again? ...

Nikolai Not playing?

Anna I'm too bored to play.

Nikolai Well then, let's have a cigarette, *mon ange.*

Dodin: (To the actress) Don't be afraid to engage your body. You have to find a way to feel her state of mind. Don't be afraid to let your head drop into your hands or straight onto the keyboard. Triletsky's agitation is intrusive, you have your own problems and he's really been upsetting you. (Assumes Triletsky's role): "Wonderful hands". He's overwhelmed; he's almost salivating at the sight of her. (Improvises as Triletsky): "There is something about her... She's unsettling... I love her". Because of her brisk responses Triletsky suddenly looks like a fool and the situation turns awkward. There is a pause just before they start smoking. Obviously he's embarrassed; he's in desperate need of a cigarette; he starts throwing himself around like an idiot. He's desperate for a smoke. He hasn't had one since early morning. By the way, that's a fact, he hasn't smoked since morning: he was busy sneaking around to catch a moment with her. His usual morning routine would be getting up, having a long smoke, a good scratch... What he really wants to tell her is: (Improvises as Triletsky): "You don't have to pretend. Just relax, pour your heart out..." When he takes her hand, Anna breaks the conversation again. (Assumes Anna's role): "What's this? My annual check up?" "I'm fine" she wants to say, "leave me alone..." (Assumes Triletsky's role): "It's not your pulse I'm after...It's like kissing a swan's down." And he kisses her hands not once but again and again. (To the actor) You can

be either playful or serious. First try to play it for real. She's really soft as a pillow, these are indeed the whitest hands in the whole country… he kisses them once, twice…(Assumes Triletsky's role): "How about a game of chess?" Chess is a legitimate reason to spend more time with her, to continue their conversation. She concedes: "For want of anything better". But there's a lot of tension under the surface. This man's been hanging around since morning; the guests have been waiting for hours; she's been delaying serving lunch past the limit of good manners… What's very important to understand about her is what is a cover and what is straight talking: which of her words are meant for him and which she simply can't prevent coming out.

Anna   Quarter past twelve… No doubt our guests will be starving.

Nikolai   Well if I am anything to go by…

Dodin: Triletsky understands – The whole waiting has been going on for three hours, but still he tries to protect her. There are dots in the text all the way. Thinking of it, the conversation goes on for quite a while. The dots always mark either an internal change provoked by something or a reaction to the partner. (Assumes Anna's role): "You, you eat all day and you're still hungry". She says this frankly but immediately changes the conversation to something else. (Assumes Anna's role): "What are you doing? What's the point of playing if you don't think? Look, think, move". She goes back to the chess game again and again. Why does she do this? Because Triletsky's constant staring makes her feel uncomfortable. For Triletsky the chess game is only a pretext to be with her, to stare at her, to breathe her in, to try to move their relationship forward. 'Look, think, move' – she means 'don't stare at me, play the game and let me think of my own things'. Because she has something very important to think about. (Improvises as Anna): "You're always hungry… the chef got drunk… you grab any half-eaten pie that's lying around… the last thing you need is another meal… small man: huge stomach!" It's obvious that she is preoccupied with her own thoughts and is just chattering on. Triletsky's constant staring is driving her crazy, she hasn't even noticed that he's already made his move: (assumes Anna's role) "Oh, for goodness' sake, get on with it." Triletsky follows his own line

135

of thought with the speech about the appreciation of food: (assumes Triletsky's role) "I don't understand you Anna. A woman of your sensibility who's not interested in food. Taste is one of our senses; it's like seeing or hearing. A discerning stomach is as important in life as..." In fact he's telling her something very important at this moment. He's telling her: 'I eat a lot therefore I'm healthy and strong; therefore, maybe, with your kind permission... Love too is one of our senses; it's our sixth sense, the one that unites all the others... Mens sana in corpore sano... Please, listen to what I'm saying...' On his part it's not small talk at all. It's a serenade of love. But to her he's a nuisance.

Anna Oh please, not an aphorism. Please!

Nikolai Why not?

Anna No aphorisms. They're banned. As are jokes. Especially yours. Hasn't anybody told you? Your jokes aren't funny.

Dodin: She has something else on her mind. He's just in her way, she thinks he doesn't understand. But she doesn't understand either why all these people are there, why they come into her house, they eat her pies. Her mind is preoccupied and she makes the wrong move on the board. But still she knows that his jokes are innuendos of love; what else could they be? We come here to the basics of this situation. The Voynitzevs have their estate, their house; this is their home but they are living on the last of their money. They live on the last pennies from the estate that will soon be slipping out of their hands. There are still the pits left but Anna knows that as soon as the estate goes under the hammer, the pits will have to go too because there are debts to be sorted out. Debts cover everything that they have. You read in today's newspaper: they killed this one, they bombed that one – it's all because of debts which they couldn't repay. Debts are all that Anna is left with. That's why she has to be smart, to wriggle out, she almost has to sell herself. There is this unspoken pact with Glagolyev and, the way things are going, she might have to marry him. She has to wriggle out of this, of course, to prevent it happening. But it was the same previously with the general: she tried to get something out of him but was left with nothing. She knows that by approving of Glagolyev buying the estate on condition that

she'll continue to live there, by agreeing to this, she has got herself into a trap! It's such a pressure, such a threat - becoming totally dependent! The conflict with this fellow, Glagolyev, is just waiting to explode... In the city she can somehow forget about all of this. We often manage to put things out of our minds when we travel abroad for instance; then we come back and all is as it was, and everything reminds us of our problems, and the anxiety consumes us. Things haven't improved; in fact they have got worse... Anna has to bear all these ugly faces again. Another one has shown up, Petrin, who can undress her with his stare. And there is Vengerovich tramping about as if this is his own home – up and down since morning inspecting everything. It's as if the bailiffs have invaded her house. But this teacher, Platonov, there is something fresh about him. There was a spark between them just before she left for Saint Petersburg, nearly a promise that they would meet in the summer; that winter wasn't the right time for romance.

Actress: Platonov is perhaps the only person that she really wants to meet again.

Dodin: Yes, parting always makes things become more significant, particularly if something was left unfinished. Imagination changes things... Anna is waiting; instead she has to watch her stepson running around with this wife of his, who behaves like George Sand.

Anna   So. Is she coming today?

Nikolai Of course she is coming. She promised, she gave me her word.

Anna   Then why isn't she here?

Dodin: (Improvises as Anna) "Platonov's not here yet. Neither is Grekova. They might be together, having fun down by the river, up in the grove?"

The Actor: Maybe the same thought has just occurred to Triletsky also?

Dodin: I don't know. We have to check this. Maybe. But his mind is not on Grekova just now. It seems to me he doesn't think of Grekova; he's totally focussed on Anna. But we still have to check this. He watches Anna. He tries very hard to read her thoughts. Maybe some reaction of hers will give him some idea.

Anna   Tell me, I'm interested, what do you think of Maria Greko-

va?

Dodin: She's not interested in his feelings for Grekova, more likely she wants to know about Grekova's feelings towards him, which will answer the question about Grekova's feelings for the one that she cares about - Platonov.

Anna   I'm asking as a friend.

Nikolai What can I say?

Dodin: Triletsky's not really answering; he's thinking aloud. (Assumes Triletsky's role): "It's true, I call on her everyday. We talk. We walk in the woods. Is it boredom? Is it love? I don't know?" What he says is that first - he doesn't know, he doesn't know what Platonov means to her; he hasn't worked that one out yet; but secondly – to him it's more important to know what he means to Anna, and she to him… We have here this baffling exchange but in fact, if we think it through, it's a very meaningful conversation. Triletsky goes even further in his admission: (assumes Triletsky's role) "All I know is that by the afternoon I miss her. I miss her terribly." At this point Anna is listening so intently her jaw has dropped. He has to remind her that it's her move.

Anna   Love, then.

Nikolai looks at her a moment.

Nikolai Perhaps. She's a nice girl.

Dodin: This pause in the middle says a lot. As if he's saying: (assumes Triletsky's role) "She loves Platonov, same as you… I'm told she misses me too… when he's not around…" Then he asks Anna: "What do you think, do I love her or not?" He's taking a risk and when Anna tries to avoid answering he says repeatedly that she doesn't understand him; he has opened his heart to her but she's not capable of responding. At this point there are plenty of dots in her lines, plenty of pauses. I'm convinced this is because he is constantly staring at her.

Anna   Oh, yes, she's nice all right…

· *Dodin:* Maria IS young, she IS a girl, there is nothing Anna can do about this. That's why she can allow herself to be a bit patronising, as we often are with young people, without sounding mean.

Anna   Does she still study chemistry?… good for her. That pointy

little nose: she'll make an excellent scientist. No, really, I like her. But I fear for her, too.

Dodin: Anna says all the nice things about Maria but her tone is so condescending. She sees her as a potential rival and she finishes her with one pitiless blow: (assumes Anna's role) "You'll keep her company, you'll fill her head with nonsense, and at the end you still won't have made up your mind. My advice would be either marry her or leave her – but nothing in between." Then she goes on slashing them both with passion: (assumes Anna's role) "Be sure to ask someone else for advice. Don't rely on your own intelligence. In your case that's the worst mistake you could make." She's simply ranting away, she can't stop herself. But where does all this anger come from, what's she on about? Here's her stepson with Sofia, Platonov with his Sasha. It's all wrong. When it comes to marriage she's always surrounded by ugly faces while the decent men go on to marry little idiots with pointy noses. Triletsky's a bit taken aback but not on account of Maria. In fact he is smitten by Anna's outburst of jealousy which he knows is not directed at him but Platonov. He understands her, he sees through her, he loves her and admires her. Her impulsive temperament charms and disarms him. She's 'unsettling'. After this long interlude they finally get to the main topic of interest – Platonov - who's a threat to them all.

Nikolai A man who sees it as his mission in life to tell women they're stupid.

Anna It's true. He does.

Nikolai He's got it into his shaggy head that Maria isn't too bright, so now she's just the object of his mockery. She's tired of it.

Anna smiles to herself.

Dodin: They can finally share something, they can go on gossiping about Platonov's arrogance, and plotting how to protect the little idiot who has fallen for him. If she's fallen for him she's not stupid, as Platonov says, she's just… a little idiot who is in love.

Anna He should be here by now. Where is he? I haven't seen him for six months. Is he well?

Dodin: This is the break-through. She's impatient, she's upset, and she's worried. This is the question that's been tormenting her all

morning. This is an intimate question. Underneath the anxiety, the disdain, the fear there is a thrill and anticipation. Triletsky can also get it off his chest; he's not hiding his own contempt for Platonov. (assumes Triletsky's role): "Platonov is always well. When is he anything else?" It seems to me, that we have a rich and meaningful conflict unfolding in front of our eyes. And not even a clue which way it could go or how it could be solved. Everything is already entangled and everyone involved has a lot at stake. I think it's a good starting point for our research to begin.

Two

Dodin: The remark '*They all sit down*' doesn't mean that we have a conclusion to the ongoing conversation, it doesn't interrupt Glagolyev's thought: (Assumes Porfiri's role) "Oh yes, Sergei Pavlovich, in our day we treated women as deities. We worshipped them like goddesses". Anna's exchange with Nikolai about the chess piece comes in the middle, while they all sit down and Glagolyev continues his speech.

Actor: But they come in and he sees Anna playing chess with Nikolai and the speech about women and friendship is directed to her.

Dodin: Of course Glagolyev has her in mind but it's not a new thought, it's part of the monologue he has already started. They've already seen each other that morning. Triletsky, Glagolyev, Voynitzev, Vengerovich, Bugrov; they've been in the house for a while, they have moved around, bumped into each other, split up in different rooms, peeped into the kitchen. Only Platonov is missing. When he comes they will greet him. But the rest of them, they have already met. They don't need to greet or acknowledge each other. The day is moving on. They hung around, walked, played, swam and still no food! Anna and Nikolai's exchange interrupts you but you're really wound up and carry on regardless: (assumes Glagolyev's role) "And what's more, we would go through fire for our friends." It's not nostalgia for the old times. He's trying to deprecate current times, including the people hanging around.

Anna   Hold on, how did that get there?

Nikolai You put it there yourself.

Dodin: Every time Glagolyev shows up Anna gets distraught: there is an issue there waiting to be solved. That's why she lost track of the game and made the wrong move. (Assumes Anna's role): "Did I? Pardonnez-moi, alors." What she says is, that it's true, that she got herself into this situation by herself, that there is no one else to blame. You can see that these are not simply two parallel conversations when Anna is talking about one thing and Glagolyev about another. There is an undercurrent and all their lines echo each other. You just have to listen to them: "...we treated women as gods...", "... you're cheating..." Glagolyev's chivalry is just pretence, he's a fake. He answers with a passionate speech about how great friendships used to be. Then Voynitzev's ironic line 'What a remarkable time it must have been' winds Glagolyev up even more. 'I have an answer to this cynical remark of yours', he's saying, and goes on to tell the story of the young man who wasn't afraid to cry at the theatre. (Assumes Glagolyev's role): "When I was young, people were not ashamed of their feelings. When you cried, you cried. When you laughed, you laughed." 'That's how we were', he's saying, 'we were capable of noble feelings, we knew how to admire, how to love and how to hate'. This is not a linguistic exchange. There is an existential clash going on here. The lines are entangled and overshadowed but the main truth is that they can barely stand each other. There are different reasons for this; there are many interests at stake. Some of them are rich, some are poor. Glagolyev's the only one from the older generation who didn't lose his fortune; on the contrary, he's increased it. He's a tough guy; he only looks small and meek. He's the only member of the gentry who is successful and is getting richer and richer. And he kept his integrity and inheritance intact.

Sergei Voynitzev Well, to be honest, I rather admire him for it.

Porfiri Glagolyev Exactly!

Dodin: The ongoing argument between Anna and Voynitzev and Glagolyev is not an argument of equals. (To the actor playing Voynitzev) You can't ignore the assumption that he doesn't have to think about money and you do. (Improvises as Voynitzev): "If we agree to live on the estate after he's bought it, he will think that we don't

have any principles". They're both under great pressure.

Nikolai (to Anna)   God deliver us from the curse of nostalgia!

Porfiri Glagolyev   When you loved, you loved. When you hated, you hated.

Anna suddenly gets up

Anna   I can't go on. Really! The smell of cheap cologne is unbearable.

Dodin: Anna is equally irritated, I think, by both Glagolyev and Voynitzev. (Improvises as Anna): "This stepson of mine, what a fool, he's just come to the estate; tomorrow it will be sold to Glagolyev and he goes around entertaining the man, having intellectual discussions with him. The idiot found himself a woman and wasted all that money (that he doesn't even have) on her, and on top of it refuses to work; being a schoolteacher is not good enough for him, you see! And this other idiot, Triletsky, covered himself all over in this dreadful cologne. I'm so irritated that I'm starting to cough, I might even choke…". That's the level of intensity that we're dealing with here. That's how hot are the emotions that have gradually filled the space. It doesn't have to be shouting, as you might think: it's intensity, passion. The heat of their emotions is very high. How will it all end up if that's how we find them at the beginning?

Day Two

Act One
One

Nikolai   Is that a reference to me?

Dodin: (To the actor playing Triletsky) You moved away, rightly so. You are hurt to tears by Anna's rude remark. She touched some nerve, something that will make you get drunk later. In addition, Triletsky put all this cologne on with good intentions. He thought that it was good to smell nice.

Actor: But he realises now that it's not the scent, it's not even him that irritates her!

Dodin: It's not him at all! (To the actor) That's what hurt you so much. She's been horribly rude and on top of that in front of other

people.

Actors start a discussion about what a cheap scent is.

Dodin: How does one know what a cheap scent is? Let's say an actor comes in the morning to rehearsal and there is this miasma around him. It means he drank the previous night, the cologne he has put on doesn't cover the smell of spirits: the smells mingle. Triletsky's scent is somewhat like that. Body odour, cheap cologne, alcohol all mixed together. But for people who are not rich and don't have refined tastes even putting a perfume on is a big deal, it's making an effort...We say, it's not real Champagne but we still call it champagne, don't we? There is similar conversation between Yakov and Lopahin in *The Cherry Orchard*...

Triletsky says the line 'What an amazing woman!' three times in the play. We have to find different ways to say it. (Improvises as Triletsky): "Amazing woman! She has only herself to blame and she doesn't even want to admit it... and why is she so cross? She's turning everything upside down."

Two

Dodin: You have to watch where their thinking is leading. Every line sets you on a particular path. Glagolyev's thinking doesn't end here. (Improvises as Glagolyev): "When we loved, we loved". Glagolyev emphasises that there is more to him than money. Triletsky's line to Anna 'I have to warn you that if you don't return immediately, I shall claim victory' shows that he can't be undermined, to protect his dignity. Despite all the conflicting undercurrents, on the surface there is a polite conversation going on. Underneath it's a battlefield; each of them is trying to hold their ground. This is very important to understand. Every dialogue is in essence an argument. And the clearer, the sharper it is made the more interesting it becomes. They converse but they also relate, they are together, they share a space. (Improvises as Anna): "This man, it's not enough that he bullies us with his money, he has to batter us with his deliberations too..." Note that Glagolyev doesn't shout, he's just thinking aloud. (To the actor) You were spot on about this. Maybe you remember

what Chekhov used to say to Leonidov: "Why do you shout when you play Lopakhin? Lopakhin doesn't need to shout, he has too much here." And he would point to his pocket. "He has a fat purse there, why would he need to shout." Leonidov didn't understand that because he believed that the role was very passionate and he insisted on raising his voice.

Anna   Say it! Say it!

Dodin: (Improvises as Anna): "Say what you want! Decent people are always idiots and the vile ones are rascals. If you're not an idiot then you're a rascal. Say it!" Anna is capable of sensing and expressing a lot of what is going on. She has this human richness about her. She says one think but at the same time manages to express plenty of other things too.

Anna   And anyway I want to listen to what my dear neighbour Porfiri Glagolyev has to say.

Anna has gone to sit opposite Porfiri Glagolyev.

Actor: She interrupts her game with Triletsky because of Glagolyev.

Dodin: That's why she goes to sit opposite him and show him that he has her attention. Meanwhile when she leaves the table Nikolai says 'That's the feeblest excuse I've ever heard. Who in their right mind would want to listen to Porfiri Glagolyev?' But Glagolyev is not offended. Triletsky's words just confirm that he's right. (To the actor) And anyway you can't offend Glagolyev. Your words can be offensive but can't really offend him. Look what the papers are writing today about Chernomirdin or some other big shot. It's impossible to hurt them. The dogs bark but the caravan moves on. Money is power. What can really offend a person like Glagolyev? It's the same in Act Two when Triletsky is begging for a loan but also trying to hurt Bugrov: (assumes Triletsky's role) "May you live for many years and die even fatter than you are… You sweat all the time, you drink, you speak in that absurd voice, your veins are sticking out like hoses. You seem to be on the way to an early grave." (Act Two, Scene One, One) Bugrov just sits and looks at him; the fly is trying to bite the elephant.

Three

Dodin: (Assumes Vengerovich's role): "The heat! Dear Lord, the heat! Is that what Palestine is like?" This is also a very interesting line. As if nothing has happened until that moment. Here comes a man for whom everything begins only with his own entrance. All that's preceded it has no importance to him whatsoever... We were rehearsing once at the Moscow Art Theatre: Vassilyeva, Smoktunovsky, Georgievskaya and suddenly the firemen poured in – simply like that, out of nowhere. How many years have passed since then but to this day I still remember this. The entrance of Vengerovich reminds me of those firemen. He comes in and sits at the piano, he can't play, of course, but he ripples the keys. (Improvises as Vengerovich): "Damn the heat, it calls to my Jewish mind a picture of Palestine."

Nikolai Owed by the General's widow, the sum of three roubles. When, pray, will the debt be honoured?

Dodin: (To the actor) I don't understand it. So much is happening here! Vengerovich, who irritates Triletsky enormously, has showed up. Triletsky can't stand Voynitzev and hates Bugrov but hates Vengerovich a hundred times more because he's a Jew. Vengerovich is like a red rag to him. Although Triletsky doesn't start talking to him straight away, he becomes visibly jumpy. So what does Triletsky do next? He begins to behave like a Jew.

Actor: Like a merchant.

Dodin: (Assumes Triletsky's role): "Owed by the General's widow..." He's like a clown. We have to find a voice for this clown-like regression. Boris Zon once told me how in high school, in year two or three, this backward child used to sit next to him – the son of a very wealthy merchant. He was three to four years older than everybody else, a big guy. When he got bored he kept calling 'Zon, Zon, Zon'. Zon would growl at him: 'u-u-u!' The guy would scream: 'Ouch!' The teacher would come and the guy would complain: "Zon insulted me."

Later in the play Platonov says to Triletsky 'The point is that we're all so much less than we ought to be' (Act Two, Scene One, Eleven). They mention how they always failed their Latin. They were no good at school. Platonov learnt enough to proclaim freedom for prostitutes

but didn't get much further with his Latin. And Triletsky – he's got only a few medical terms to show off. Platonov often teases and abuses him about this. There must be reasons for that. In your probing so far I can't see these reasons. Why Platonov has chosen this particular guy to abuse systematically is not clear to me so far. In your studies of Platonov there was a glimpse of an explanation: perhaps Platonov wants to shake up this guy, wants him to change, to become a different person. As for your studies of Triletsky, there wasn't anything there at all. On the surface he's a witty guy with no obvious reason to lack confidence. But still there are plenty of questions here. What kind of doctor is he? Why does Platonov mock him all the time? Why is it always for being a bad doctor, for not taking his profession more seriously? At the end, announcing Sasha's suicide attempt, Triletsky says 'Platonov's favourite topic. My shortcomings as a doctor. I called this morning. It was pure chance. Pure luck. I happened to pass by the house.' Platonov replies: "I've never had much faith in medicine but from now on - Hippocrates to Triletsky - that's the extent of deterioration." (Act Four, Nine) Triletsky's excitement at this sorry event is very interesting. (Improvises as Triletsky): "You lucky bastard, thank god I popped into the house! If I hadn't caught her she would've been dead by now!" How proud he is of himself, how pleased to emphasise his ability. Despite the impression that he doesn't care, that entire matter about his professional competence is important to him.

Let's go to that line: (assumes Triletsky's role) "When, pray, will the debt be honoured?"

Actor: Glagolyev continues his lecture on how much better people were in old times but in Vengerovich's presence it now sounds as if it is addressed to him.

Dodin: Maybe. Or perhaps Glagolyev is simply developing his thoughts. Vengerovich came into the room as if there was nobody there. Glagolyev continues to speak as if nobody has entered. This is also a reaction. It's not that he hadn't noticed. This is a way of noticing, by pretending that you didn't notice. Control is one of Glagolyev's faculties. For instance, he wrote this article and gave it to Triletsky to publish under his name. He knew that, on the one hand, Tri-

letsky's such an idiot that he wouldn't realise the danger and has nothing to lose. On the other hand, the idiot that he is, he would be pleased to have his name at the head of that article. Feeling superior gives him power over people.

Actor: What could this article have been about?

Dodin: Some machination most likely. Nowadays they constantly accuse businessmen in their dirty dealings of hiding behind figureheads. I was told about this article proving that Chernomirdin is holding the majority of the shares of GazProm. When they asked him at a press conference whether it was true, he replied 'it's unethical even to answer a question like that'. He didn't say that it's unethical to be asked these questions. He's no fool... Glagolyev feels he's better than the rest of them on many levels – as a rich man, as an aristocrat, as an anti-Semite. The relationship between him and Vengerovich is hostile but the way they behave is a different matter.

The Actor: To pay much attention to Vengerovich's arrival is below Glagolyev.

Dodin: Of course. Glagolyev can't allow himself to be polite with Vengerovich and Bugrov because they will be rude to him anyway. There is only one choice left, to be rude himself to neutralize their rudeness. In the play it's all linear but in fact everything is happening at once. On the page it's a sequence so you tend to play it in turns. You have to allow all the moves to take place simultaneously. Vengerovich's reaction comes in the middle of everything else. No turns, it's one integral action there.

Porfiri Ah yes, ladies and gentlemen, if you'd lived through the old days, then you'd sing a different tune.

Dodin: (To the actor) It has to be clear, what Glagolyev is answering to. You leave the impression that you are continuing the ongoing conversation, which is fine. But what exactly is everybody saying in that particular exchange? (Improvises as Glagolyev): "I'm not saying that the present is bad; I'm just saying that the past was so wonderful. From that perspective the present doesn't look very good at all..." (Improvises as Voynitzev): "I read books. I used to love to read old newspapers. You don't have to tell me how it was in the 70's. You don't even have to tell me about the 50's. I know well how it was. As

for why I can't be entirely happy with my Sophie, my father is to blame. He left me with nothing although I still respect him very much. You're the one buying our estate and not the other way round." (Improvises as Triletsky): "I don't understand, why nobody ever listens to what I'm saying in this house. Why everyone has a say but me...You better pay me what's due, as you pay this Jew here..." (Improvises as Anna): "Oh shut up, I can't hear what people are saying because of your ranting." (Improvises as Triletsky): "Because you don't even look at me and I'm watching you all the time." (Improvises as Anna): "Sergei, do your dear stepmother a favour, just give this idiot three roubles to stop him shoving his emotions in my face." (Improvises as Triletsky): "You'd better pay up; you only respect people that fleece you, don't you? I love you and you don't even look at me." This argument can go on endlessly.

Actress: Is the gesture of getting his wallet out and paying Triletsky three roubles a kind of reproach to Anna for wasting the money?

Dodin: I don't think so. Voynitzev is not in a position to reproach her; it's her money after all. Mummy's paying... He simply has a very serious attitude towards money, it's a big deal to reach for his wallet, taking money out of his wallet is all he does these days. Triletsky's reaction is more interesting. Once he gets the note in his hand he starts clowning around, he even slaps Abraham on the back: (assumes Triletsky's role) "*Merci*. Isn't this the way to live? Fleecing innocent women at games?" If it was up to Vengerovich or Bugrov they would have put the note quietly in their wallets and that's it. Not Triletsky though and he gets an immediate reaction form Vengerovich: (assumes Vengerovich's role) " What can I say, Doctor? Like a true Jerusalem aristocrat." Not a true aristocrat, but one from Jerusalem – quite...

Actor: Triletsky has to react to this.

Dodin: Of course, that's why Anna interrupts immediately with 'Don't start, Triletsky!', because he's ready to go... So she changes the conversation and we move into a new round. (To the actor playing Glagolyev) The moment she addresses you, the expression in your eyes must suddenly change. Glagolyev was talking in her presence but not necessarily to her. Now he's talking to her directly. It's

an entirely different situation.

Anna *(to Porfiri)* So, Porfiri Semyonovich, it's your view, is it, that women are superior beings?

Porfiri Indeed.

Anna Tell me: this must mean that you enjoy great success with them.

Dodin: This exchange is so intimate it's close to the point of being indiscreet. This is a game. Anna lures him into a certain situation then she begins to evade because one more word might push him to offer his hand and heart openly in front of everybody. There is nothing to stop him, nothing to embarrass him. It's the proper thing to do. His intentions are honest, his motives are good: (assumes Glagolyev's role) "In women, Anna Petrovna, I find all the virtues in the world."

Anna You find them, yes. But are they there?

Dodin: Meanwhile Triletsky is exasperated by the way they've excluded him from their conversation. He can see what exactly is happening between Anna and Glagolyev. If he could he would have hit them with the violin he's holding...

Anna Nikolai, please, put the violin down.

Porfiri Anna Petrovna, one need only look at you.

Dodin: (To the actor) You are just answering her question: you don't even dare look at her or you have to declare your love. That's what he had in mind a while ago when he said, 'When you loved, you loved.' (Improvises as Glagolyev): "We weren't afraid to admit our feelings. When the woman that I love stands in front of me and asks, 'do you love me', I'm not too shy to answer honestly. (Assumes Anna's role): "But is it true?" 'Are you really sure, she's asking, or you just want to believe it?' (Assumes Glagolyev's role): "I'm absolutely sure... one need only look at you." Anna can't get out of this that easily. Her little game has paid off. Obviously we are talking about passion here. Glagolyev is hit so hard that even the thought that Anna might belong to somebody else can give him an apoplectic stroke.

Sergei He's a romantic.

Dodin: Another interesting line.

Actor: I think he truly believes that Glagolyev is a romantic. Didn't he say before, 'When I was young, people were not ashamed of their

feelings'?

Dodin: Sergei and Anna, they live on his money. Thinking that he's a romantic, to a certain extent acquits them in their own eyes. If Anna goes on to marry him, everybody would understand but nevertheless, she has to find another excuse to save face. All this puts pressure on them. The gutter is just one step away. (To the actor playing Sergei) When Glagolyev says of Platonov, 'He exemplifies the modern vagueness, the modern malaise. No point, no purpose', he's blaming you for living on his money, for being ready to exchange your stepmother for money. This is another round in the ongoing altercation and a pretty nasty one. That's why Glagolyev has the right to say that you don't know how to love or to hate. He has his reasons for thinking that.

Actor: I can't openly confront him, even if I want to. I'm in the position of a dependent.

Dodin: Of course, and Glagolyev knows it. He knows that when he says something they will listen. (Improvises as Anna): "Shut up you idiot, I can't hear what people that matter are saying." Everything Glagolyev says about the superiority of women is not just a romantic speech... It's not pure polemic. There isn't a single empty word here. From the very beginning they are all discussing the important thing, the only thing that they will go on discussing until they destroy each other.

Porfiri   Very well, take romance away, but what then do you put in its place?

Anna   Let's not argue, my friend. I don't like to argue. We know better. Isn't knowledge always an advantage?

Dodin: Glagolyev is saying, 'You must allow me to love you, you must allow large, generous, free feelings to exist. I can openly ask you: come to me. Why can't you reply: 'I'm coming'. Are you afraid?'

The actress: My answer is: romance or no romance, at least I'm wiser now...

Dodin: (Improvises as Anna): "Let's not turn everything into a polemic, my friend, she says. I'm no good at arguing. The important thing is that we now know where we stand, don't we?" This exchange is so tense that when Glagolyev comes to the brink of popping the

question, she cools him down with a very straight answer: (improvises as Anna) "I'm not giving myself up that easily as I once did with the General. I've already tried this, thank you." 'Isn't knowledge always an advance', is a very firm answer. (Improvises as Anna): "If we're so clever, let's slow down and be clever, then all the rest will be fine. I didn't say anything wrong. I didn't say no."

There is a moment of silence. Then Anna turns to Nikolai.

Anna   Nikolai, please. Put the violin down.

Dodin: She's going through enormous emotional transitions. They are like powerful tides swaying her this way and the other: she shouts, whistles, laughs, cries. That's why they are all drawn to her. When she laughs Glagolyev's temples start to pulsate. She attracts men and she knows it. It's not the first time she's using her power – and she'll say it later – it's not her first time at all. And she'll say it again the moment Sasha shows up, when everything is just about to happen between her and Platonov. This is a woman of enormous experience. And there is also wickedness in her. She will say to Platonov in Act Three, 'You look like an actor playing the part of a lovelorn… I tell you, that sort of thing does nothing for me.'(Act Three, Five) 'Put the violin down!' – Triletsky's jaw must have dropped, so harsh and sudden is her command.

Porfiri   In fact, Platonov put this rather well. I remember he once said: "We have advanced in our attitude to women. But the effect of our moving forward has been only to achieve a retreat."

Dodin: Let's explore "we have advanced". (The actors try to say the line with an emphasis on "advanced"). At first sight he says, 'we know more, we got wiser', echoing Anna's line above. But suddenly Triletsky is laughing most sincerely. (Dodin starts to giggle and all the actors begin to laugh too).

Nikolai   *(giggles)* Yes, well, that sounds like pure, unadulterated Platonov. What was he? Drunk?

Actor: There is obviously a double meaning to this line.

Dodin: 'We have advanced' means we've dragged women in the dirt. 'We have advanced means we're no longer ashamed of openly treating them as an object of our sexual desires. It's clear what was the meaning behind that phrase of Platonov – all we think of is how

to drag a woman into our beds! That's why Triletsky's laughing, he finds this funny. (The actors argue about the meaning of Platonov's phrase.) I think there are many things at work here. I also think that Chekhov has picked up this moment with remarkable precision. This thought could have only come into the head of a true womaniser who on top of that is admired by everybody for this. 'Sounds like pure and unadulterated Platonov' – there is a touch of admiration in Triletsky's words. As for Anna she nearly got off her chair at the mention of Platonov's name: (assumes Anna's role) "He is fond of these pronouncements, isn't he?" The words of her beloved are like music to her ears. (Assumes Anna's role): "But he knows they're not serious". 'He's not trying to humiliate me like all of you', she's saying, 'he didn't even come here. He's fond of a good phrase that's all...' He did seduce somebody last summer though, and completely lost his head. Even in the winter he wasn't ready yet to switch to me. It was meant to happen now but he doesn't even bother to come by. Glagolyev's so hung up on me his eye balls are going red and Platonov's staying in his bed until midday, that's how much he cares...'

Anna Comes to this, what do you think, my friend? What is your view of Platonov?

Dodin: (Improvises as Anna): "Comes to this... You're our expert in sexual relationships, give us your opinion." (Assumes Glagolyev's role): "Platonov, madam?" Of course, he has an opinion, he has an answer to this question, he has answers to all the questions in the world: (assumes Glagolyev's role) "I see him as a hero of a Russian novel. And as you know, Russian novels are the worst in the world... he exemplifies the modern vagueness, the modern malaise. No point, no purpose." This is a continuation of the previous conversation; his take on the present state of society. But he's also saying, 'Of course, I know about the situation with Sofya... it's all messed up and extremely confusing... people don't know what they are doing... that's what I call vagueness and our clever Platonov exemplifies it.'

Actor: Has Glagolyev noticed how Anna shook her wings at the mere mention of Platonov? Isn't he trying to put down Platonov a bit in front of her?

Dodin: Of course, he is. And he puts him down very well. (Impro-

vises as Glagolyev): "Don't put your bets on Platonov, he's the one you can't rely on…" (To the actor) You're right, Glagolyev has spared his most malicious sting for Platonov. (Improvises as Glagolyev): "I remember he once said… I talked to him… I listened to what he had to say… I know what kind of man he is and I'll never forget it." This is a highly interesting point in the exchange, the way Glagolyev quotes Platonov. I was visiting friends in Salzburg some time ago and I met a young man there. I asked him what he was doing in Salzburg. He said he was studying in the Salzburg Conservatoire. I asked him why there. He said that he had started his studies in Russia, first in Saint Petersburg then in Moscow, but there was nobody there to teach him. Anyway there is no one that can teach you Russian music in Russia, and no one can seriously believe that there is, and it's even ridiculous, and any way there is no point studying at all because the most important thing is to look after yourself. 'Do you read books', I asked him. 'No, I don't', he said, I used to like it as a child, but now I don't. It only breaks you and distracts you from the important thing of looking after yourself.' 'But still, you go to the Conservatoire, don't you', I asked. 'I do but the conditions are really good, I can attend the lectures I choose, I spread myself evenly, that way I can learn something.' He was talking without stopping to think even for a second, without showing emotion, very rationally. He was lying about the books because to build that kind of argument one obviously had to have read some books. But there he was in front of me a truly contemporary representative of the young generation. Still I wouldn't advise anybody to have anything to do with him. As for his music? I might've tried to listen to it once, but it's unlikely I would have had wished to a second time.

Porfiri   No really, my point is this: he's a brilliant man…

Anna   He's kind.

Porfiri   Oh yes.

Anna   He's decent.

There's a silence.

Dodin: Glagolyev is waiting. (Improvises as Glagolyev): "What else do you want to know about Platonov?" In some ways Glagolyev's characterisation of Platonov is very accurate. Platonov is earnest in

many ways: from his love for Sasha to the dread that he might end up living with her; from the pleasure he takes in repairing the bird-cage to his terror that it's all that he will be left to do; from his love for teaching to the embarrassing realisation that he's ONLY a teacher. He's all messed up and confused.

Anna Why isn't he here? Nikolai, go tell Yakov to fetch him.

Dodin: Here's a glimpse of Anna's true feelings. (Improvises as Triletsky): "She's been waiting. That's why food hasn't been served yet and we are all starving…" Triletsky doesn't like to be told what to do so his irritation shows when he bumps into Bugrov arriving.

Four

Nikolai And here comes our grocer friend, puffing like a steam train…

Dodin: Triletsky can't exit quietly, like a servant, so Bugrov's entrance comes conveniently for him. Bugrov's entrance is also interesting: "Such heat, my friends! It must break soon." He pretends that the only reason he's coming here is to find some shade from the heat. He pretends that nothing much is happening and he's not interested… such heat… he sits and covers his face with a handkerchief. The exchange between Sergei Voynitzev and Bugrov, 'You haven't seen Sofya, by chance?' looks casual but is also important. Sergei hasn't seen Sofya for a while. They've all been talking about romance and no romance, love and no love. It has made him rather unsettled. He can't stand being away from his Sofya for long, he loses his calm. He has to see her all the time.

Bugrov Sofya?

Sergei My wife, Sofya Yegorovna. Have you seen my wife?

Dodin: Vengerovich rushes inside because he can see Voynitzev is annoyed and ready to go: (improvises as Sergei) "My wife's name is Sofya Yegorovna! And since you've come here you'd better know the name of the mistress of the house!" Vengerovich can't stand Sergei's lecturing but another important event is happening right there – he's seen Platonov and Sasha arriving in Russian national dress.

Platonov has such a powerful turn of phrase! For such a young

writer as Chekhov it's such a confident piece of dialogue!

Platonov   The end in sight! At last! We have arrived at last! Your excellency!... Yes, we have finally made our escape. From hibernation.

Dodin: Platonov has a happy home but here everything is different… His transition from his own house to this manor is not that simple…

Actor: He had to repair the birdcage; Sasha had to go to church; it's not that straightforward. Were they really held up or did they take their time, delaying as long as they could?

Dodin: Of course they did. Something happened between him and Anna. It has to be continued. There is an obligation there so one would need a serious reason, like a broken cage, to be held up on their way. Sasha knows about this thing they had. She knows that her husband is not the steadiest of characters, he won't do anything underhand but still… They weren't intentionally late … That morning they simply went on doing things around the house as if Anna hadn't arrived yet. The cage needed mending – they mended it. They had to book a service in the church – they booked it. Platonov didn't rush Sasha, Sasha didn't hold Platonov up.

Actor: They saw the lights in Anna's manor the previous night, didn't they?

Dodin: Yes. (Improvises as Sasha): "If you want you can go to say hello." (Improvises as Platonov): "I don't want to. They might have gone to bed already. And Kolya's expecting me to play with him a bit. And I don't have a second pair of trousers. You can't go twice to people's houses wearing the same pair of trousers. I'd better keep these for the formal lunch…" The life they lead in their own house is very different.

Actor: He has his complexes.

Dodin: Platonov also had an estate once. It was smaller but he lost it. Now Platonovka belongs to somebody else. Sasha says, 'Misha, go into the room'. Not the house but the room. That's all they have, two rooms – one is the classroom, the other one they live in at three of them with their son.

Actor: Do they know about Sofya, maybe Yakov had told them…

Dodin: I think they already knew about Sofya. There were letters, there was gossip…Glagolyev could have told them after returning

from Saint Petersburg. He went with Anna to Saint Petersburg to ne-
gotiate the sale. Glagolyev kept on pressing Anna until she agreed to
the sale, then they made the announcement. The announcement
has been already published. Vengerovich walks around the house
examining everything closely because he intends to buy it. He
knows that Glagolyev will be his main rival. Glagolyev also knows
that Vengerovich or someone on his behalf will bid against him.
That's why he's publishing this article to expose Vengerovich's
machinations. It's a dirty game. Glagolyev's writing an article expo-
sing him as an underhand player because Vengerovich doesn't even
have the right to take part in the auction and is using other people,
namely Bugrov. Glagolyev is using Triletsky, a known truth-seeker, to
sign the article. (Improvises as Glagolyev): "I have nothing to hide!"
(Improvises as Vengerovich): "Whatever, but if it was written by a
Jew they would have said "Jewish tricks". Anna knows about the article. She had read it, she was sent the cutting from the newspaper.
This is to prove how many things are intertwined here. Platonov
knows about Voynitzev's marriage to Sofya. For him it's such a blow
from the past. He has something going on with Anna and knows Sofya is coming too. Has she changed? What will happen? Voynitzev
has married Sofya and moreover he has graduated from University.
Now he's coming with Platonov's former lover on his arm. Platonov
was once her hero and mentor in earthly matters. Once in New York
I was very keen to meet an old friend of mine, a childhood friend but
he declined. A great guy but somebody got it into his head that this
wasn't the right moment and it was better to avoid encounters that
might not be to his advantage. That's rubbish, of course… But it's
easy for me to say it… Although I don't know what his situation was
there, he might have been perfectly happy without meeting me…
(Improvises as his friend): "Why come here and bother people, he'd
be better off staying in Saint Petersburg for good… what's the point
in coming, calling people, let's meet…" The important question is
how much of all this can Anna sense? Of course she has some understanding because I think she's a very clever woman. For Platonov to
continue his flirting with Anna in the presence of Sofya would be somehow… uncomfortable.

Actor: Just to make it clear about the article. Triletsky has signed it. Has he made his own deal with Glagolyev or was Triletsky *pere* also involved?

Dodin: He signed it himself. It was easy for Glagolyev to poison him because he can't stand Vengerovich anyway. Maybe he told him let's 'write it together' then wrote it himself and made Triletsky sign it. That's why Triletsky is angry with him. First, it's a dangerous thing that Glagolyev dragged him into, and secondly he's left looking like a fool because he didn't even write the damned thing. So he says that people shouldn't listen to Glagolyev. (Improvises as Triletsky): "Who in their right mind would want to listen to Porfiri Glagolyev? If you do you immediately get yourself in trouble." On the other hand Triletsky is vain, he's flattered to see his name in the newspaper. He's even asking around, 'Have you seen my article?'

Let's go back to Platonov. He's is under great pressure. (Improvises as Platonov): "I'd rather Anna stayed in town for good, Sofya died young and Sergei emigrated somewhere..." That's why he does everything in such a pedantic way. It took time to repair the birdcage. Sasha went to church, all the usual business but the tension underneath is palpable. (Assumes Platonov's role): "The end in sight! At last!"

Actor: New round of the game.

Dodin: They're even dressed up...

Actor: That's because she doesn't have a decent dress...

Dodin: It's a nice costume. But of course, it would be better to have a proper dress. It's the same with Platonov. Apart from his black winter trousers he only has one other pair, for the summer. With the black pair he goes to work, goes fishing, plays with Kolya; they're all worn out and faded.

Anna   You're a ruthless man, Platonov. To have made me wait so long. You know how little patience I have... Dearest Sasha!

Dodin: Anna's outburst has left Sasha completely ignored, as if Platonov has turned up alone. We have to understand the power of emotional release in Platonov's words 'We have arrived at last! Your Excellency!... Sasha, say hello.' It's an achingly intimate exchange. It's obvious that they have this thing for each other but feel uncomfor-

table in front of Sasha, in front of all these people... so he has to include Sasha immediately... The remark is *'Anna kisses Sasha'*. (Improvises as Platonov): "See, people are pleased to see us, they kiss us, it's all so different here..." (Assumes Platonov's role): "For six months we have been starved of the pleasures of parquet floors... The two of us slept through the winter like bears, huddled in our den... *(Platonov goes round shaking hands)* Greetings, Porfiri Semyonovich..."

Sergei   *(to Sasha)* Good Lord, Sasha, you've filled out. Do the two of you do nothing but eat?

Platonov   And don't tell me this is Sergei Pavlovich! Changed beyond all recognition. Where's the long hair? The tunic? The piping treble of boyhood?

Dodin: These exchanges are pregnant with meaning. The fact that Maman is breathing heavily in Platonov's face is deeply hurtful to Sergei. Only in Act Four he will get it off his chest and say, 'He's not yours any more, he's not, and she's not mine!' They all know everything; there aren't any idiots there. Even talking about the forthcoming sale in Platonov's presence puts everybody in a difficult position. These are not simple encounters.

Actor: Is Platonov envious of Sergei?

Dodin: It's not only envy, there's humiliation too. What is somebody else's success, it's my humiliation.

Actor: But Platonov has to hide his envy.

Dodin: Of course. He might even go on joking about all this. People always try to hide their feelings even when they tell you, 'Oh I do envy you', they're still trying to hide what they feel. There are many ways of doing this. Everybody has their own. Platonov hears what Sergei is saying to Sasha. He loves Sasha's roundness but when people point at it and call her 'fatty', it drives him crazy. He likes Sasha, he likes that she's so sensual, he feels comfortable with her. But when other people called her "fatty" his guts start churning.

The nature of Platonov's relationship with Sasha is very interesting. I'm convinced that when they are on their own they feel great with each other. It's only when a third party is present that complications begin.

Anna   Come, sit down. Tell us what's happening.

Dodin: There are some formal phrases that are expressions of politeness only. And there are others that have been flogged to death. 'How are you?' – you don't expect much of an answer. But here we have, it seems to me, a different situation. (Improvises as Anna): "Sit down… Tell me… Sasha's not in my way and I am not in her way… I'm genuinely interested in your life…Sit down". That's what Anna's trying to say. Instead of answering Platonov gets into a quick exchange with Sergei: (improvises as Platonov) "Instead of staring at us you'd better look at yourself. We teach children, that's what we do. Now they know that three times three is nine. Two years ago they didn't. I've worked out my own system, two more years and they'll know the entire multiplication table. It won't be that easy to lie to them when they know their maths. But what's the point telling you this. You don't want to hear it."

Actor: Platonov greets Glagolyev too, but he doesn't react.

Dodin: At least there are no hugs or kisses, no verbal exchange. And by the way Glagolyev is watching all the time, he's observing… As for Sergei he's offended by Platonov's words but he pretends he's taking it as a joke.

Sergei   *(laughs)* He always does this. Always!

Dodin: They say that very shy people sometimes overcome their shyness by being overtly rude. They call it Mayakovsky's syndrome. Mayakovsky behaved so badly, they say, because he was abnormally shy. There is a touch of this when Platonov begins the speech about human flesh.

Platonov   Sasha, do you recognise the smell… Flesh, human flesh! I'd almost forgotten.

Everyone laughs.

Dodin: There are many smells mixed it that room – from Anna's perfume to Triletsky's unbearably cheap cologne. That's why they laugh, because it's the second time the issue has come up. But Platonov gives it a different turn: (improvises as Platonov) "It smells of real people, it's not like the stale smell of boiled potatoes that is in my house. It smells of life, real life."

Platonov   The matchless smell of humanity! It seems as if we have been deprived of it for over a hundred years. The interminable win-

ter! And there – look – remember, Sasha? – the chair in which I sat last year, discussing the meaning of life, day in, day out, with the beautiful Anna Petrovna...

Dodin: There is another subtext here. Platonov is saying to Sasha, 'Do you remember, six months ago I spent my days and nights with Anna discussing matters of life and death... but that's all it was... nothing more... you understand?' He's not very convincing; there's a silence in the room; they stop to listen to him. Platonov has this tendency of confronting difficult points when they occur but not always successfully ... Anna fills the pause.

Anna   Was the winter really that bad?

Dodin: "Winter is a time for sleep, only after that does life begin. Nearly every year, when the days begin to lengthen, my mother-in-law calls us on the phone to say: 'Congratulations. As from today the day is getting longer'. It only expands by 20 seconds but still... You've barely seen the day getting longer and then it starts getting shorter again..." Platonov is hesitant, he has to find the right tone with Anna. She has openly shown her affection for him; she's not hiding anything. For him it's more complicated. (Improvises as Platonov): "It seemed we had something but now it turns out that we didn't. No, we did! Anything could have happened. Just one more night, but then you left. The farewell ball, the dance, things were warming up. Now we are back to square one..." For Anna it's much more straightforward. (Improvises as Anna): "Tell us what's happening? You didn't for a second think of me, did you? You fell into your wife's arms and that was it?" His answer is an attempt to reassure her.

Sasha   We got by. It was boring, of course.

Platonov Boring? The word 'boring' could never begin to convey it.

Sasha   It was fine.

Actress: She says her husband is lying. (Improvises as Sasha): "He has this tendency of saying things about our life that are not true. It was a bit boring but that's why we're so glad to be here."

Dodin: Platonov intercepts. (Improvises as Platonov): "If you're so keen to join the conversation, my dear, let me tell you, it wasn't just boring, it was unbearable... I missed you... Anna... You're open, I'll

be open too"

Platonov   Just to see you, Anna Petrovna, after such an eternity, after such an Antarctic boredom, just the sight of you: yes, that is compensation enough!

Dodin: And he's back into the game they used to play, mixing true and false, the game they both used to like so much.

Actress: Then here's your reward, "…have a cigarette".

Dodin: Yes, it's the right tone, you can allow yourself to be both playful and sincere.

Sasha   You got here yesterday?

Dodin: It's unclear why you're asking. It looks as if Sasha's only being polite… But we know they had a conversation, they saw the light but weren't sure. It's an entirely legitimate question. Sasha is a rather straightforward girl. She knows her husband has weaknesses that are largely compensated by his virtues. She tries her best to smooth these weaknesses over, to understate them, and very often she succeeds. She's a true mistress of her house. Even when the situation is disastrous she continues to behave blamelessly. Overall she's the only lucky person in their family and everybody loves her - a truly sober individual in the best sense of the word. Later it will transpire that she's also a person of the highest dignity. Because when it becomes clear that Platonov is a coward, she won't be able to live either with or without him. Then she has to die because she loves him. She will poison herself and Platonov will be shaken to the depths of his soul by the news of her suicide. There were other things there too: the broken hand, the horror he went through, the close call with death, but the important thing is the loss of Sasha. They have a deep and very earnest relationship. That's where the drama comes from. If he had been married to a housekeeper there wouldn't be a drama. But the realisation that in this world that's all there is for him – Sasha and their home - makes him feel bad and behave awfully, and it gets worse in the presence of other people. That's what brings him down. Sasha is a person of staggering dignity. And she never compromises it. That's the reason why Osip respects her so much. He knows them all, what cowards they are, all of them. The general's widow – she's a queen, but mean as a snake, and this one – she's

a saint. (Improvises as Osip): "If only I'd met a couple more like her I would have become a monk".

Platonov   I saw your lights on at eleven but didn't dare call.

Dodin: Platonov worries that Sasha will say too much so he interrupts – 'I saw your lights on at eleven' – it's the same information; he just puts it a bit differently. (Improvises as Anna): "For God's sake, why not? I've been going mad here waiting and waiting". Next comes the remark *'Sasha whispers in Platonov's ear'*. What is she whispering?

Actress: I've just remembered that we have to congratulate Sergei for the wedding.

Dodin: You didn't forget. You know that it's the first thing to do. But for some reason your husband is talking about everything but this, and you discussed it on your way here... (Improvises as Sasha): "Why can't you mention the wedding?" So now Platonov has to.

Actor: Voynitzev is expecting first of all to be asked about the wedding. It's even better that Sofya is not present, it's already a bit awkward as it is.

Dodin: Yes, so Platonov has to go into overdrive. (Assumes Platonov's role): "Forgive me – my God! You should have reminded me before. And you, Sergei, you didn't say a word." He's looking for excuses everywhere. (Improvises as Sasha): "Here he starts again saying God knows what... It's getting embarrassing." Sasha wants to congratulate Sergei properly, in a civilised manner...

Sasha   And I forgot as well, Sergei Pavlovich. Many congratulations. I wish you a lifetime of happiness.

Platonov bows.

Dodin: A spare reaction from Platonov. Voynitzev is on the alert. Marriage is a slippery matter, it can be easily turned into mockery. (Assumes Platonov's role): "I would never have expected it. The ultimate act! And performed at such incredible speed!" It's the beginning of Platonov's assault on Sergei.

Platonov   Well, forgive me: I've known you 'in love' once or twice, you could say I've rarely known you out of it, but it's the marriage bit that's new. All I hope is you haven't married a stupid woman. That's the worst kind of hell.

Sergei   Well…

Platonov   Have you found a job?

Dodin: It's like an artillery attack. He picks up on every word Sergei says. He undermines Sergei's admission that he's in love. (Assumes Sergei's role): "It's true. One day in love, the next day married. It was quite a shock." (Improvises as Platonov): "You've been in love so many times, plus now you're married… it's not that big a change… one more verb give or take…" Then he attacks the marriage itself. (Improvises as Platonov): "You've got yourself a censor, that's what marriage is – censorship. The dumb censors are the worst… now you have to work… ". Voynitzev knows very well that he's a coward, he's living off the last of Anna's money but refuses to work. He's trying to cover up and retaliate at the same time. (Assumes Voynitzev's role): "To be honest, I have been offered a post in a school, but the pay's very bad." 'It's not that simple', he's saying, 'I have some offers here and there, but I'd rather go for something more serious…The school's not my cup of tea really…' He's really pushing Platonov's buttons. It's like saying to a struggling fringe actor that you've been offered a role at the National but you're not really sure if it is the right career move and so on… Platonov has barely managed to get a job as a village teacher not even at a proper school…This is the very first moment in the play when something dark breaks loose in Platonov's heart. We can see glimpses of the so-called "Platonovesque character", it's like a small eruption. (Improvises as Platonov): "What a coward! Anna will have to go to bed with this son of a bitch because of you… Does your new bride know about this…she was an idealist, she should know better… Three precious years you've wasted and now… look at the mess all of us are in".

Platonov   Ah yes, perfect excuse. 'Pay's bad, can't do it.' What? Three years out of university is it, and now – what – you'll hang around for three more?

Dodin: The scandal is ready to blow when Anna interferes. She doesn't want to listen to highbrow arguments. She obsesses about one thing only – why was Platonov so late? (Improvises as Sasha): "We were busy… family life takes time. It's not like in your manor where servants take care of you – off to the party… our life has routine…we

don't do spontaneous things… it's for you… we mend birdcages, we go to church…"

Actor: Why's Glagolyev entering into this exchange? 'Why on Sunday', he asks?

Dodin: The conversation got to a quieter stage. They're talking about going to church and so on, about all the right things. Glagolyev is also a churchgoer, he just wants to remind them, there aren't that many churchgoers around. There is a pause after Sasha says that it was for a memorial to Platonov's father that she went to the church. Sasha's words are a tune from a different world. It doesn't mean this rougher world is completely alien to the people gathered here but they are preoccupied with other things just now. Then this reminder of Platonov's dead father calls for our empathy. Everybody has forgotten about this death. But Sasha hasn't. It's his father's name day and Platonov has to somehow observe a state of mourning. It's very interesting how cleverly Sasha navigates and brings things in…

Actor: Platonov didn't go to church with her.

Dodin: No. He doesn't go to church, only Sasha goes, that's how they've settled this. (Improvises as Sasha): "That's the reason we couldn't come earlier." It's just an answer for Anna. Anna will later say that she'd completely forgotten about Sasha's existence. But Sasha exists and the routine of life exists – the washing of nappies while Platonov played with Kolya; that also exists. Anna has to hear about it now, so when later she dismisses it as if it never existed, it tells us a lot about her. We often prefer to pretend that we don't know about certain things. Unwillingly they got themselves into this conversation about Platonov's father. Sasha treats her husband like a good teacher treats a bad pupil – talented, much loved but bad. (Improvises as Sasha): "He can really be an angel at times but he's so embarrassed by it." To Glagolyev, who got caught in the middle of this conversation, the mention of Platonov's father reminds him that he's going there too. Old people don't like talking about these things. (Improvises as Glagolyev): "Time flies! It seems like it was only yesterday. That's life. I'll die too and not even a dog will notice. But life is stronger than death… We had good moments with him… It often

happens, you kind of want to keep mourning but memory brings the good moments to mind. (Assumes Glagolyev's role): "A great man, your father."

Actor: Why does Platonov get so agitated Why this outburst? It's been a rather formal exchange so far?

Dodin: Yes but it's turning into an intimate one. A whole life story suddenly comes pouring out, a very painful one. Platonov parted with his father when he was a teenager. They barely spoke to each other during the last three years of his father's life, they were enemies. (Improvises as Platonov): "He lost all the money, didn't leave me a penny...and never admitted what a coward he was ".

Platonov He considered me a worthless person and I considered him a fool. What I can never forgive is: this is a man who died reconciled to his own stupidity. Well now.

Dodin: It's an outrageous thing to admit your abhorrence for a dead father. It puts such pressure on everybody around you. Glagolyev argues sharply with Sergei but is always rather cautious with Platonov. That guy in Salzburg I told you about, I didn't feel like arguing with him. He would have taken any reaction on my part – admiration, indignation or outrage – as a proof that he was right, that I belonged to another generation. He already knew all about me. That's why I was very cautious. I'd say, ' I see... I see... interesting...'

Actor: I think Glagolyev is even a bit scared of Platonov.

Dodin: That's what I mean. He's always cautious with Platonov. That's why he doesn't like him. He respects him but he doesn't like him...

Actor: Glagolyev had had a talk with Triletsky about that article, maybe he went to talk to Platonov too.

Dodin: It's possible.

Actor: Perhaps Platonov guessed by the style of writing who the real author of the piece was.

Dodin: Platonov would never have taken part in Glagolyev's machinations. If he wanted it he could have written and published his own article. In any case it's possible that Glagolyev had visited him with a purpose and not just for a casual conversation. He says later, that he visited Platonov and was greatly impressed. There is something else – Glagolyev appreciates strength. In the decisive mo-

ment he will come to Platonov and say: "Possibly you may think this is a strange enquiry, but upon your reply depends my whole future." (Act Three, Ten) Platonov had already told him the truth a couple of times before.

Actor: But why is Platonov jumping at everything Glagolyev says?

Dodin: Platonov doesn't trust him. He knows him. He has always tried to avoid confrontations with Glagolyev. He's the same. He didn't start it; Glagolyev started talking about his dead father. Once they move away from the neutral ground they both try to stay on, the hidden animosity shows up (alternately improvises as Glagolyev and Platonov): "Great man, your father"… "No, he wasn't"… "I respected him"… "I didn't"… "It's wrong to speak ill of the dead"…"Of everybody either nothing or the whole truth, and listen; you put this thing in the paper; shame on you too, Sergei, for allowing all this to happen." The confrontations are close and the motives are mixed. We tend to forget about this when we act: we know the stuff, every character's pre-history but it's somewhere there… We have to constantly remind ourselves it's all here, in this space. The question about the estate is constantly present; it never goes away regardless of what they talk about. It is the same in real life: wherever you put your finger you touch a wound.

Actor: Reading the play I always ask myself what happened to Platonov's estate Platonovka?

Actress: Platonov asks Kiril Glagolyev at some point 'Is it true that your father wants to buy Platonovka?'

Dodin: And Anna will say to Petrin that Glagolyev had brutally deceived the General by buying out all his shares.

Actor: Perhaps Platonov hates Glagolyev because he was the one that robbed his father?

Dodin: It's possible. It's a fair point.

Actor: But then would Glagolyev have dared to visit Platonov on the matter of the article?

Dodin: Yes. We are often drawn to the people that we don't have the best of relationships with; we want somehow to make them better, otherwise we worry they'll get even worse. Glagolyev is a decisive man. He doesn't shy away from problems. He knows that expo-

sing the fraud can make Platonov his ally. (Improvises as Glagolyev): "You always stand for the truth. Sign this letter." (Improvises as Platonov): "I'm not signing your letter; I can write my own."

Actor: Then Glagolyev's speech that in his times people were better, more generous and forgiving is may be a move to get Platonov on his side…

Dodin: Of course, of course. (Improvises as Platonov): "You were forgiving but we are not, we can't forgive…" This is a valid interpretation. Everything is pregnant with pain. Once they start talking of his father, the tension immediately escalates. It's because Glagolyev ruthlessly robbed his father despite the fact they were friends. Glagolyev's the first one to say nice things about Platonov's father but they sound like mockery. And he does it in front of everybody. That's where the power of Platonov's explosive reaction comes from, and not because he's an eccentric and can't control his outbursts. The pain and the hatred are so intense it's impossible not to explode! They all ask: 'why is he so highly strung, so provocative, why does he stick his nose in everybody's business?' He doesn't want to but he has to, he is forced to. Somehow Platonov's union with Sasha offers him a way out of all sorts of trouble. For Voynitzev the marriage to Sofia is also an escape from all sorts of trouble. (Improvises as Voynitzev): "I'm happy! To be precise, not entirely happy, but in general – very happy! She makes me forget about everything! She's above everybody. She's not like my stepmother. I have a wonderful stepmother, I love her very much, but it always scared me to think that I could have a wife like her. Sofya is not like Anna, she's superior, she has pride, she's different…" (Act One, Twenty two)

It's such a complex set of ideas and emotions. Perhaps it's enough for one day? Your brains must be boiling?

Actors: They are…

Actor: Still, why is Platonov's entrance so bold, so blown out of proportion? Perhaps he feels how complicated the situation is which he's coming back to, that makes him tight, jumpy…

Dodin: Of course.

Actor: The intricacies, the danger mesmerise him.

Dodin: Of course. While at school he's completely consumed by his

work. But a lot of gossip's going around. And he's drawn back to the life that he should have broken away from. At least he tried to.

Actor: During the winter he doesn't have to live a lie.

Dodin: During the winter he doesn't have to lie to himself nearly as much. But look at the things that have been stirred up now, look at what is coming... And everybody's reaching for him, everybody needs him. Let's break for lunch and in the afternoon you'll practise on you own.

Actor: And with the orchestra?

Dodin: And with the orchestra. The first half of the day we'll work together, the second half you'll go on practicing the things that we've come up with. The serious work with the text of the play doesn't undermine the importance of the music and dance. The better we understand the complicated nature of their lives and the pressures they are under, the clearer it will become why from time to time one feels the urge to shout, to sing, to blow a tuba or saxophone or break into a dance or whatever. We'll have an hour of dancing every day. Valery Zvyozdochkin has selected the material that will help you feel things through movement – an hour of speech warm up and an hour of dancing. By the end of the week you have to be able to perform bits of dancing regardless of where and whether we'll use them or not – perhaps just to understand what kind of dance is appropriate and would fit in. You will continue to play different roles to give you some freedom and we will energetically move forward.

Day Three

Act One
Ten

Nikolai   Maria Yefimovna! What a pleasant surprise!

Dodin: At the point of Maria's entrance the tension is very high. Triletsky has asked did they see the article which he wrote, Vengerovich confronted him with the accusation that he didn't write it. Triletsky is offended but that's not Vengerovich's point. He merely stated the fact, he's just saying to Triletsky, 'You didn't write anything...

stay out of this.' The important thing for Triletsky is - what will Sasha think of him; what will Platonov think of him. Platonov was invited to sign the article himself but he refused. Now it's all in the open, and in front of everybody – Vengerovich, Bugrov, Glagolyev. It's humiliating – for Anna, for Sergei, for Platonov himself. Platonov is embarrassed for Triletsky too. The situation is humiliating for everybody. Bugrov and Vengerovich put them all in an awkward position. That's the degree of tension when Maria comes in. It's true for Platonov too. One might be in conflict with somebody but if they have to share being humiliated with them in front of other people that's absolutely unbearable – I'd like to kill you, to strangle you and hang myself too. Triletsky must have broken into a sweat when Glagolyev's authorship of the article came out. Imagine how he explodes: (assumes Triletsky's role) "Maria Yefimovna! What a pleasure! What a surprise!" Still, somehow I don't understand what exactly is stirred up with Maria's entrance? Why's Platonov jumping towards her? Why is she so flustered, embarrassed?

Maria sits in an agony of embarrassment. Nikolai sits next to her.

Maria   If you don't mind, I prefer my hand not to be kissed. I can explain. I find it embarrassing.

Platonov has got up to greet Maria.

Platonov   Greetings, Maria Grekova, let me kiss your hand.

Maria   I've just said no. *(Maria snatches her hand violently away.)* Why don't you listen?

Actor: I think that Maria thought about it longer than all of them - should she come here or not. They all had a history with Platonov and he had treated her badly. But despite this she is desperate to see him. She's also flustered by the fact that everybody will see her as Triletsky's future bride…

Dodin: So what?

Actor: They all know everything.

Dodin: And so?

Actor: Triletsky had promised that Platonov wouldn't be there but she wants to see him, she can't wait to find out and when she sees him - naturally she's a bit agitated …

Dodin: And?

Actor: In his conversation with Anna, Triletsky is adamant that Maria is not coming, because Platonov would be here.

Dodin: Why did she come then?

Actor: Because she had some hopes she'd see him.

Dodin: She came because she knew for sure that Platonov would be there. And I'm convinced Triletsky didn't promise anything. (Improvises as both Maria and Triletsky): "Will he be there or not?"... "I don't know, Maria Yefimovna, I can't be responsible for his actions..." "If he's there I'm not going!..." "I can't promise you anything. It's not my decision..." "I'm definitely not going and that's it. You can tell them it's because of him.-.." "There is nothing I can do, he might or he might not... Oh, here he is!" For Maria it's at the same time a shock and a release. (Assumes Maria's role): "...I prefer my hand not to be kissed!" She's perspiring profusely. She can't take her eyes off Platonov; she's in love to the marrow of her bones. And it drives Platonov crazy: because she's in this state; because it's so foolishly obvious; because he has to respond somehow to this. At the same time he's touched by her feelings but everybody is watching him.

Maria You only tried to kiss me because I said I particularly dislike it. You do everything you can to annoy me.

Dodin: Platonov didn't do or say anything that could reduce her to tears. But she is neurotically in love; it's the desperation of a lonely person who in the middle of the desert has fallen in love with the only person available within a thousand miles. She can't stop thinking of him day and night, night and day...

Meanwhile Triletsky's desire is to draw the conversation away from the newspaper: (assumes Triletsky's role) "What a pleasant surprise!" But she can barely hear what he's saying, her ears are ringing, she's crazed, like all of them by the way... (Improvises as Triletsky): "It's great that you've come, we'll change the subject of conversation now and we won't return to it ever again..." Everybody wants to move away but the entrance of the love-struck Maria makes them feel even more uncomfortable. Even Nikolai's father is caught off guard: (assumes Ivan Triletsky's role) "My goodness, so this is Maria Grekova. Forgive me, I scarcely recognised you." (To the actor) You always read this line in a deep tone since you want to sound solid. Why don't you

try imbuing your voice with that edge brought about by the uneasy situation: he hasn't read the newspaper, he doesn't understand who did what, he's confused: (assumes Ivan Triletsky's role) "My goodness, so this is Maria Grekova..."

As for Maria, she's out of breath. She loses control totally at the sight of Platonov. (Improvises as Maria): "Don't kiss me... you don't love me... it's insincere... if only you loved me, but you don't... why do you always do the opposite of what I want...you do everything you can to annoy me". She's cringing inside, because kissing her hand would be a sign of love.

What a great playwright Chekhov is! When Platonov says 'You obviously consider me unworthy', she answers "I don't consider you anything – I don't know whether you are worthy or unworthy but you're insincere, aren't you?"

Platonov   Am I? Really? What makes you think that?

Dodin: (Improvises as Platonov): "How do you know? Maybe I am moved by your emotion?" Strangely enough, Platonov is dragged into it. (To the actor) When somebody gets an electric shock just from your look, from touching you, you can't remain unaffected. That's why you'll even kiss her later. It won't happen immediately, just gradually. And when he kisses her later, she believes that he's sincere, because he kisses her sincerely. With this young creature in front of him, trembling from love, he can't help but be moved. When somebody looks at you with total adoration it moves you. It lifts you up in your own eyes. It excites you. At the same time it's all happening in front of an audience, in front of his wife and everyone... But still he feels like talking to Maria because nobody has ever loved him like she does. Just one move and she'll faint in your hands and you can do with her whatever you want. (Improvises as Platonov): "You, silly girl, why do you want this? Why do I want this? Why am I such a fool, all the time wanting something?" (To the actor) Sasha can see this. It's not the first time something like that has happened to her husband. Everybody else can see it. Triletsky knows about it. He will say in Act Two: "What can I do? What am I meant to do? Pursue the man with a club?"

Our characters lose their money, their estates and their power – only passions are left. As they say, decadent times. More and more

passion completely washing everything away.

Nikolai   Platonov, please, leave her alone.

Dodin: (Improvises as Triletsky): "Just stay away from her, you always get her into this state, she's shaking all over. Can't you see, she's trembling?" (Improvises as Platonov): "Why do I have to... In a moment, I will. But first, about the bed-bugs..." Platonov's absurd inquiry into Maria's latest scientific experiment 'adding to the sum of human knowledge' brings Maria to the verge of a nervous break down. She's like a exposed live wire . (Assumes Platonov's role): "And now you seem to be turning red. What's happening? Is this another experiment? Or can it be the heat?" Maria is the type who blushes from love. Her cheeks reveal her sensuality. Platonov is immediately overwhelmed but her emotion also makes him angry. (Improvises as Platonov): "For Gods sake, you're flushed as if we're already in bed. We are not even on the way..." Still, he can't stop talking, as if he's begging, 'Let me talk to you a bit... Why are you so cross? Will you ever forgive me? If you love me just tell me so... No need to be cross."

Maria   Why do you do this? Why do you always do this?

Platonov   Do what? I don't do anything. Isn't it for me to say: why do you always get so angry? Why are you upset with me?

Dodin: (To the actress) You don't have to shout. Grekova's not arguing with Platonov. As much as she can, she's trying to sort out her relationship with him. (Assumes Maria's role): "If I'd known you'd be here I wouldn't have come. *(She turns to Nikolai)* You promised! You promised he wouldn't be here." (Improvises as Platonov): "Really? How did you know I wouldn't be here, Nikolai? It's no good lying. Are you about to cry? Good, that will make you feel better, you're already too flushed." You can see that he's not mocking her. He's just being sucked into her mood, he's infected... that's his reaction to her. Grekova is just about to collapse when he says: "Cry, Cry...". I remember I had a teacher in the nursery. She used to tell us: "The more you cry the less you wet yourself".

Eleven

Dodin: It took us a while but we can see now that Maria's arrival has stirred everything up, like a whirlwind, like a hurricane. Every-

body is about to join in with their own agenda; it's turning into a major scandal. Triletsky is also moved by the girl's state. (Improvises as Triletsky): "Being in love with you is not a reason to mock her...any more of this and you'll have me to deal with." (Improvises as Glagolyev): "It's cruel, Platonov. You are being cruel." Anna's trying to calm them down. (Assumes Anna's role): "Ah, welcome, Maria Yefimovna. This is such a pleasure... We see you so seldom. Please, let's sit over here." (Assumes Glagolyev's role): You must apologise, Platonov... Apologise, damn you." (Assumes Sasha's role): Why? Why do you do it?" You can see that it's all happening at the same time.

Twelve

Anna   I must say, Mikhail...
Dodin: (Improvises as Anna): "If that's progress, thank you! It gives me a headache. I'd rather let myself go in somebody's strong arms and not feel anything, just pleasure... I can tremble like this. I'm young, I'm young too, but I'm getting old with all these burdens and complications...I can't allow myself to be so frank and open...
Porfiri   Sometimes you go too far.
Anna   It was wrong of you, Mikhail.
Platonov   And haven't I said I was sorry?

Thirteen

Sergei comes from the house, followed by the student, Isaac Vengerovich, and by Sofya Yegorovna. Sergei bursts into song.
Sergei   (sings)
    She's on her way and now she's appearing
    She's on her way and now she's here...
Dodin: Even when we just read through the play, we must try to follow all the lines and connect all the dots. Otherwise it will be like starting from the beginning every single time. Voynitzev storms in enthusiastically at the worst possible moment and in the most inappropriate mood. This is Sofya's much anticipated appearance – she

comes in and starts praising the garden. Maria has just rushed out with Nikólai close behind. Everybody's attention has been stretched like rubber, out, in. They're back now welcoming Sofya. But then Nikolai comes back shouting that he's fed up with women. He's been humiliated by Maria's outburst, he had to run after her in the garden, he left her to her own devices and is back very annoyed with all this and himself. They've started a new conversation and he's finishing the old one, but he doesn't know that. The remark is *'There is a silence'*. Why?

Actor: They have been anticipating the meeting of Platonov and Sofya all morning: they're waiting for the scandal to happen.

Actress: Nikolai has interrupted their conversation, they note the irrelevance of his interference before resuming their conversation.

Dodin: Possibly. Sofya says: "What a ravishing garden!" Glagolyev says: "…Your beautiful wife promised me that you will all come over to my place on Thursday…I assure you my garden is infinitely superior…" Why do they all go quiet, there is something here… Perhaps they all have noticed that Sofya has recognised Platonov. (Assumes Glagolyev's role): "…My river is deeper, and I also have exceptional horses." *'There is a silence'*. I wonder if Anna understands what exactly is happening here?

Actor: No, she knows nothing. She hasn't heard about this liaison of Platonov. She wasn't present at the conversation with Voynitzev when Platonov said that he had known Sofya a long time ago.

There is a silence

Anna Silence. Another fool has been born.

Dodin: She can obviously see that everybody is preoccupied with something. The important point comes when Glagolyev tries to explain to them how to get to his estate and mentions Platonovka.

Actor: But if Anna doesn't know about the affair, why does it look as if she's also taking part in their little game to reveal nothing about Platonov for as long as possible?

Dodin: She is taking part.

Actress: She realised what's in everyone's mind in that moment of silence. She can see how Platonov sits, She can see how Sofya looks at him…

Sofya   Platonovka... It still exists? I once knew its owner.

Dodin: (To the actress) Why so lifelessly? Nobody would listen to Sofya like this. Look what she says and how she says it. She's been overwhelmed by the company of Isaac; she's been overwhelmed by the beauty of the garden; they are all waiting to hear what she has to say. With her entrance all previous conversations become immediately unimportant. She's not loud but she's assertive and a bit rude to Platonov. (Assumes Sofya's role): "It's you. You've changed". When he says, 'You always said you thought I would turn into another Byron... What happened? I'm a schoolmaster', she answers, 'I don't believe you.' Then she goes over all of Platonov's failures in the past five years since they parted and she's really hurtful. So Sofya is quite a character, you have to find the right voice for her.

Sofya   You got your degree?

Platonov   No. No. I quit without it.

Sofya   But you're still...

Platonov   What?

Sofya   Human? You're still a human being?

Platonov   Well, loosely.

Fourteen

Pavel Shcherbuk arrives, calling back from the veranda.

Dodin: The important thing here is that Shcherbuk is another of Anna's creditors. She's obliged with every single one of them to dance to their tune. None of them shows much consideration for her: they lend her their money and they want a hundred per cent return. Shcherbuk's so loud and coarse, he antagonises them immediately. Sofya's doesn't want her hand to be kissed by him: (improvises as Sofya) "Thanks but... you don't have to". First, he might smell unpleasantly, second, kissing hands is not in vogue and is not progressive. Sofya holds her hand out for a handshake but Shcherbuk turns it over to kiss it. (Improvises as Sofya): "Don't kiss it... you might just as well bite it." (Improvises as Shcherbuk): "That's a bit rude... I carried your husband many times in my arms. (Indicating Platonov). And look at this lad whom I also knew in his boyhood. Look at him

now!" Shcherbuk provokes them all. To Platonov: "Why aren't you in the army"; To Triletsky: "My God, I hope you haven't been consulting that appalling quack." To Sofya: He stuck his wide-open mouth right in her face to demonstrate how as a toddler Sergei had broken one of his teeth. Triletsky takes any attack on his professional abilities very badly. The truth is he's not really good enough as a doctor; he doesn't have it in him. That's why saving Sasha makes him so proud of himself, although all he did was to stick two fingers down her throat to make her throw up. Shcherbuk never pays him properly. This was a common occurrence; doctors were often not paid for their services. Chekhov mentions this several times. The rich, they exploit everybody but when it comes to calling the doctor they don't bother to pay. They treated doctors like servants. That's why Triletsky immediately gets angry. He says to Platonov: "Platonov, you're the closest, hit him on his bald patch." They are arguing for real. I saw this once at the Kirov Theatre, when a man was hit on the head. Our seats were close to the aisle and a couple was sitting in front of us: the man was completely bald and the woman very beautiful, with a lovely coat. After the one-minute call people started to settle down and falling silent. Then I saw this woman coming down the aisle: she looks around, comes closer, stops by the row where the man was sitting. Then she bends suddenly, takes off her high heel shoe and hits him straight on the head – bang! A loud crack; blood running down his skull... She just puts her shoe back on and calmly walks up the aisle and out. A pause, but this is the fifth or sixth row. Everybody has seen it; another second of silence and then... an explosion of hysterical laughter. At this very moment the conductor is stepping onto the stage, he thinks they are laughing at him - perhaps his trousers are undone. He turns round to check. Another explosion of laughter. That was a scene straight from *Platonov*. That must have been the man's wife, he was with another woman. At least that's how I read it. (To the actor) You carry on, hit him on the head, everybody will interpret it in a different way. (Improvises as Shcherbuk): Enough! Go away!... Don't push the sleeping lion..."

Sasha Father, you mustn't fall asleep. It's rude.

Dodin: It's amazing how round after round the action never lets up.

Petrin is reading the paper aloud; Shcherbuk is telling him off; Trilet-sky is shouting at Shcherbuk; Sasha is shaking her dozing father; then Petrin attacks Platonov – the pot is really boiling. Petrin's line is the most interesting one here. (Assumes Petrin's role): "Petrin, Petrin! Who is Petrin? Only a man with a law degree, that's all. Yes. With letters after his name. Yes. A man now approaching his seventh decade, That's all." (Improvises as Petrin): "I'm not a joke… Everything here is paid for with my own money. In this house everything belongs to me and yet I have to come here as a guest!"

Petrin Setting out on his way, a man can take one of three paths. Go to the right and the wolves will eat you. Go to the left and you will eat the wolves. Go down the middle of the road and you will eat yourself.

Dodin: He's bursting with frustration. He can't eat the wolves, they've eaten him already and he can't do anything but eat himself! Anna is like a red rag to him: he stumbles around her and all he sees are his wasted millions.

Actor: Whose side is he on then?

Dodin: Anyone's. He says to Glagolyev: go on, marry her, if that's how I will recover my losses. He's ready to take anybody's side just to get his money back. The Voynitzevs, they live, eat, drink, travel all over the world, wed, marry – he pays and gets nothing! (Improvises as Petrin): "I'm reading aloud! I'm in my own house! I'll do as I please. They write here about people like you, in debt up to their neck. Your Excellency, I beg you, give me my money back, even just a fraction of it, I beg on my knees. The money's mine. Mine! What does it matter how I got it? You'll sort out your problems with your husband in the grave. I got my money lawfully! (To Glagolyev) I beg you, marry her… I would have proposed myself." When Platonov is drawn into the argument he immediately gets very agitated too.

Platonov I care little for your experience. Homespun wisdom cuts no ice with me. Least of all when it comes from my father's friends.

Dodin: (Improvises as Platonov): "I deeply distrust all your aphorisms on serious matters; I distrust everything you come up with yourselves. (To Glagolyev) You're also my father's friend. I don't trust you either. You always utter noble phrases; you might not be capab-

le of true villainy but still… Why do I have to trust any of you, why do I have to believe in your nobleness when you all gorge yourselves from the same trough like the vilest swine?"

This is a powerful thought. That's how deep Chekhov's analysis is. We can't simplify, it's all there, in the play. Do you remember that the main criticism of our production of Fonvizin's *The Infant* was that we debased the good characters. Here we are.

Actor: When he says: "Thank you for your frankness. I admire honesty in a man." Is he frank himself?

Dodin: It's not that simple. Getting into a confrontation with Platonov makes things worse. It's better to stay above it. Glagolyev has his way with Platonov. He knows how to handle him, to gently manipulate him. There is always something calculated when people ask you to tell them the truth. Actors do this all the time: "I was awful today; wasn't I? Scold me, criticise me…" The expectation is that you'll say, 'No, not at all.' And if you say, 'Frankly, it wasn't very good', then people get upset. Glagolyev asks: "Does that mean you have no respect for me?" Platonov gives him a frank answer.

Actor: One has to be very gullible to believe in Fonvizin's 'wise old men' or guys like Glagolyev.

Dodin: (Improvises as Platonov): "You have to be very naive to believe that in the midst of all the filth that we all live in one can remain pure and noble. You live with these people, you are friends with them… so, please, don't take offence but…"

There is a silence.

Anna   These conversations always end badly. Platonov, say hello to Isaac Abramovich Vengerovich. He's a student.

Dodin: Anna must have said this because Glagolyev turned pale after hearing Platonov's words. Glagolyev is generally acutely self-centred. He's passionate, self-centred, defensive… And the fact that somebody is gathering compromising information on him, that they are trying to expose him, hurts him very deeply. He could have easily had a stroke there and then. Too many things were piling up on him. And he never lets anything go. None of them ever let anything go. Actors are the only ones that let things pass unnoticed here and there.

Actor: Triletsky behaves nobly with Anna; he's trying to save her and he gets insulted for his pains, much more so than Bugrov or Vengerovich.

Dodin: Anna is trying to counteract this. She introduces Isaac who, she believes, is the safe option. Platonov is also pleased to get out of the awkward exchange with Glagolyev. (Assumes Platonov's role): "Lucky man! I'd give anything to be a student again. I give you my hand. Or else give me yours." He is sincere now, he's thinking of Sofya when he was a student. (Improvises as Platonov): "I wish I could start everything all over again..." He's so relieved to move away from Glagolyev that he misjudges the new situation with Isaac.

Isaac I never shake hands with people I despise... I speak as an honest man who has nothing but contempt for mediocrity.

Dodin: Vengerovich *fils* repeats word for word what Platonov had to say about the older generation. Suddenly Platonov finds himself in the position Glagolyev was just in. (Assumes Platonov's role): "Ah, very good, excellent. If I didn't think it would make you big-headed I would say I was delighted." But of course he's hurt and becomes very pale. Isaac is defending his father; it's a noble and sincere act, and although Vengerovich is not bothered by Platonov's insults, he's proud to have a son like that.

Actor: Isaac wasn't there during the confrontation between Platonov and Vengerovich: he's not reacting to it. He was in the garden discussing serious matters with Sofya.

Actor: Maybe I've told him everything about Platonov at home?

Dodin: You didn't tell him anything. It's all been going on for years. The son grew up observing his father's relations with Platonov and the other members of the gentry. This is simply the first time that he finds himself in society as a grown up, a student, and he knows what to say, he's learned his lesson. He's an adult now. I still remember some of the names of my father's enemies I heard as a boy. It was discussed at home but nobody knew that I knew. When we sometimes talk with my mother about this, she's surprised that I remember. 'It can't be', she says, 'you were only three years old then!' But I do remember because when you are very young you notice many things and they affect you deeply.

We are confronted again with a situation when things that have been buried for years and years suddenly break through. This confrontation didn't start yesterday. It's only now that Vengerovich has got enough money and power to hire somebody to beat the hell out of his long-standing enemy. That's all. The times when Platonov could abuse him or hurt him are, luckily for him, long gone. It's all in the past. Now he can pay for Platonov to be maimed. But he had to show submission for a very long time – half a life. That's why his son has the right not to shake Platonov's hand. Platonov has nothing to say about it because Vengerovich *fils* is right. (To the actor) In your eyes Platonov's a disgrace to everything, even to the university uniform you share. The uniform is to show that you are a student and not to flaunt it about the village, turning into an anti-Semite on the way. You're just honest.

Platonov All students are honest. A dishonest student would be a rare thing indeed. Won't you give me your hand?

Isaac I don't dispense charity.

Nikolai hisses.

Dodin: Triletsky wants to stop this conversation.

Actor: I thought he wanted to prevent a full-blown scandal.

Dodin: No, he's hurt and insulted as well. Vengerovich *fils* is telling Platonov all the things that apply to you too. On top of it all he's Jewish and the son of a publican. Triletsky can be as outraged as he wants at Platonov, but when he's insulted by such people as Isaac, Triletsky's on his side. A real fight is looming here.

That he has to be defended by Triletsky hurts Platonov even more. (Assumes Platonov's role): "We're talking about manners, not charity. Do you so despise me, then?" But Isaac doesn't stop the assault: "I despise you because I loathe dissembling, I loathe vulgarity and I loathe buffoonery." It's a very tough time for Platonov. I hope I don't have to go through a morning like this. (Assumes Platonov's role): "I haven't heard a speech like this for years. I used to make them myself. And with the same conviction." (To the actor) A scene just like this rises in your memory, but instead of Isaac, it's you confronting somebody else. It's so painfully familiar, you could faint on the spot! (Improvises as Platonov): "Once I was a master of scattering… it's a

pity these are only words... just pretty words... a drop of sincerity wouldn't hurt." Platonov's trying hard here to hold on to something. (Improvises as Platonov): "I used to say them with conviction but these are just imitations. Poor imitations!"

Although Platonov says: "I can't get enough (of this conversation)", it has to be admitted that Isaac got to him. It's a very strong claim that Vengerovich *fils* is making here. And it's an important moment because later in the play things will come up that will discredit him to a certain extent. Now we can assume that finally a positive character has emerged in the play. He says the things good characters say – all the right stuff.

Actor: It's also important that Sofya is observing this too.

Actress: And Anna.

Dodin: Of course, Anna, and Sofya.

Actor: Everybody's here, including Vengerovich *pere* .

Dodin: Later it will take Platonov an enormous amount of energy to reverse everything in Sofya's eyes and, how shall I put it, make her suffer for all this. On some subconscious level there is this craving for revenge. And until Sofya is forced to admit that she's fallen even lower than him, Platonov's soul won't find rest. Platonov is wounded, humiliated and cannot reconcile himself to this.

Fifteen

Osip appears

Osip   Your Excellency, I am delighted to congratulate you on your safe arrival. I wish you everything that you would wish for yourself.

Everyone laughs.

Dodin: It's not very clear what you mean here.

Actor: Osip's been around the estate since early morning. He's seen everybody coming in and out of the house and he wants to go inside as well. Stumbling into Vasili gives him an excuse to go in.

Dodin: What kind of excuse is that – stumbling into Vasili?

Actress: We have here a small bomb waiting to go off – first, a peasant is not allowed to enter the master's house without permission. Second, Osip is not aware of this: he thinks it's all right to do so. He

has just come back from one of his long trips. Anna is making a point of not noticing him because they have had an argument.

Dodin: It's his beloved lady's birthday. He puts his best clothes on and comes to the house. It has nothing to do with Vasili. He just walked past him determined to give his 'welcome' speech to Anna.

Actor: Why the laughter?

Dodin: Do you remember the retired colonel who once came to the Academy to give us a lecture on Stanislavski. Everybody laughed because of the absurdity of the situation. Osip's entrance is absurd in the same way. Osip is not afraid. Why should he be? They should be afraid of him - he's the brigand. (Improvises as Osip): "I wish you all the best, dear Anna Petrovna. As for our quarrel, I didn't take it seriously, because you were in the wrong. If I had changed I wouldn't have been able to love you. I visited many monasteries as you suggested and I realised that it's not for me. If I became a monk, I wouldn't be able to love you."

Anna *(to Osip)* Tell me just how much of our forest did you steal this winter?

Osip A few trees only. Three, may be four.

Everyone laughs.

Anna How could you afford that watch? Is it gold?

Dodin: That's right, he almost goes to sit next to her. This is their conversation, these are their jokes. Anna pretends to be cross with Osip but he has an effect on her - he amuses her, he takes some of the tension away.

Osip May I kiss your hand?

Anna Of course.

Osip kisses her hand with his lips.

Dodin: She's condescending but still enjoys it. They all watch, all kinds of emotions are in the air: embarrassment, intrigue, curiosity. They've all heard about her messing around with Osip but instead of innocent fun, now that it's thrown into their faces, it looks more like witchcraft.

Actor: Doesn't Osip give it all away with that proprietary attitude! I've seen it happening many times in real life: people are having a nice party and then just one word, one smile and instantly the sec-

ret is out and everybody knows about it. Can't she just throw him out?

Dodin: If she loses her nerve and asks him to leave, the situation will become unbearable. How can you throw out a man with whom you have had an intimate relationship? In Chekhov's *Duel* the inspector says, 'I demand two more dates'. (Improvises as the inspector): I won't allow you to treat me like a lap dog: today you want me, tomorrow you don't. That's ridiculous. We will do what I say..." Osip is not in a position where he can be thrown out. On the other hand, Anna is very strong, so strong that in Act Two she'll command him and he will obey: "When Platonov comes out of the school, fire a warning shot. Fire in the air to let me know he's back." (Act Two, Scene Two, Nine) (Improvises as Anna): "Then I'll think what to do with you." She has to have much strength of character to hold him on such a tight leash. She finds a way both to release the tension and undermine Osip's claim.

Anna   *(to Osip)* Tell them in the kitchen to feed you. Look everyone, see how his eyes light up.

Actor: This is the first time Osip makes his claim on Anna Petrovna.

Dodin: How do you know whether it's the first or second?

Actor: Because he's all dressed up, with a gold chain.

Dodin: They used to dress up for special occasions. Let's look at some photographs. They are all properly attired, jackets and all. That was the code.

Actor: But isn't he acting slightly strangely?

Dodin: He behaves very appropriately – he came to congratulate her on her birthday. Nothing unusual about that. (Improvises as Osip): "I saw her when she was down. I'm a man and she responded to me. She's not distant like the village girls that I go out with, she's all energy and passion; we even bathed together in the river once." They had some moments of fun together. Osip has this strong proprietary sentiment. He will later take great pleasure in telling Sasha about his relationship with the General's widow, because what's the point of having a fling with a woman and not telling anyone else about it. Your approach to Osip is a bit naive. Anna had some good

times with him, I don't know how far they went, you have to decide this for yourself, but they had a fling that he can't forget and neither can she. Osip is his own man. He has his own business, he cuts his own deals directly with Abraham Vengerovich. He is a working guy.

For Platonov, who has just had such a clash with Vengerovich *fils* before Osip's arrival, this is a chance to distract everyone's attention.

Actor: The moment Osip shows up, Platonov practically throws himself at him.

Dodin: That is another interesting thing that we have to explore here.

Osip kisses her hand.

Osip   Why are you holding on to me, Mikhail Vasilich?

Platonov   Because I don't want you to go. Ladies and gentlemen, it's my pleasure to introduce to you one of the most interesting living carnivores in the contemporary zoo.

Dodin: Here's an interesting moment: Platonov is really jealous of Osip. (Improvises as Platonov): "Nothing bothers him, even people laughing at him: he does what he wants." (To the actor playing Platonov) You always wanted to be like that but never had the nerve. Some of them know nothing about Osip. Triletsky is meeting him for the first time but Platonov knows him well. Osip used to go to Platonov's house where Sasha used to feed him.

Platonov has this strange chemistry with Osip. Osip touches a nerve in him in the same powerful way as Sofya a while ago. Platonov is suddenly transformed. He becomes agitated, provocative to the extent that they all think he's going a bit crazy. Platonov launches into a hysterical attack on Osip…

Platonov   By the way, just asking, but why aren't you in prison at the moment?

Osip   Everyone knows I'm a thief, but they can't prove it. And the law says you can only be sent to Siberia if there's evidence. So that's it - that's the problem with the ordinary Russian peasant. So cowardly, so stupid, so ignorant that he can't be bothered… to get himself organised to build a case against me.

Dodin: Platonov dreads prison. He was involved in politics once but abandoned it because he was so afraid of being jailed. He hates and

admires Osip's arrogance. (Improvises as Platonov): "What a smooth talker he is for a crook! I do something slightly wrong and agonise over it for weeks. He has everything mapped out and gets there with his own brain, the animal that he is. That's Russia for you! Even animals have theories. I'm not like Osip, because I'm not an animal. But if you're not a villain, you are a coward. If you don't dish out abuse you get abused yourself: that's the damned alternative. And Osip: he dishes it out and he's proud of it. And he's not the only one here, Vengerovich is the same". Platonov is unstoppable, the tension rises and we're again in the middle of a scandal.

Abraham   Please. This is no longer funny. *(Abraham gets up and changes his chair.)*

Sergei   Calm down, Mikhail. *(to Osip)* Osip, get out of here.

Dodin: (Improvises as Voynitzev): "Out! You're getting on Platonov's nerves."

Actor: Osip tells this joke about the parrot – is he mocking Platonov?

Dodin: No, he's joining Platonov in his assault on Vengerovich. Osip can't stand Vengerovich: he's a worse criminal than Osip by far but considers himself an honest man. In fact, Osip doesn't have any attachments: he's a truly dangerous man. There is just this weakness for this lady here, who has messed up his mind. He's really a criminal; he can kill without a thought. He's used to harming people but, like everyone of us, he has his infatuations. He wouldn't go and maim Platonov in front of his wife. But he has no shame. He doesn't know what shame is. (To the actor playing Osip) You mustn't paint him in romantic or sensitive tones. Anna is interested in him because, from all the scum that surrounds her, Osip is the only one that doesn't bother to hide it. They're all petty, lying bastards and he's not afraid to say who he is. And he sees and understands everything. (Assumes Osip's role): "There's not a lot of kindness in him, is there? To Mikhail Platonov, everyone's an idiot. Everyone's a fool." (Act Two, Scene Two. One) That's Osip's verdict on Platonov. (Improvises as Osip): "He's not stupid but he's not a good man. Insulting everybody, hurting everybody, and so hung up on the ladies. Salivating over this one then that one. If you want her take her, that's my motto. There

are some things about him I respect and some which I despise. But as for the General's widow, he won't get his way with her" And when Sasha tries to tell him that he's going a bit too far, Osip gives a most inspired excuse to Sasha: "Saint Alexandra, what did Platonov do? Say prayers, light candles to find a wife like you?" (Act Two, Scene Two, One) Osip has his own view on life. Love will destroy it. He will decide to turn up in daytime in the village which practically amounts to suicide. (Assumes Bugrov's role): "In life, one mistake is enough. He was killed near the well. A group of peasants got together and beat him to death." (Act Four, Four) No one would have expected such a thing from Osip but that's the strength of Anna's spell.

Actor: He was involved in the profession of killing anyway.

Dodin: It's not a profession. I mixed with people like that in Siberia. Osip is a free man: one can as easily fall in love with him.

Actor: But he thinks his life is tough, always secret, always in hiding.

Dodin: It's a better way of playing him than as a romantic, Robin Hood-like character.

Actor: I read recently an interview with of one of today's assassins. They asked him did he kill in Afghanistan. 'Of course', he said, 'if you don't kill, they kill you.' When asked what made him kill a civilian, he said, 'It's the money, but it's also the thrill which Razkolnikov felt.'

Dodin: That's different, some clever talking, nothing more. Dostoyevsky doesn't explain anything if you haven't read the book. If you look in the eyes of paratroopers you can see it. Some of them have sensed what freedom is and they know – everything else is just words. Some years ago we were driving across the taiga and a boy by the road stopped our car. He was sitting there with a small bag in hand trying to hitch a lift. One hundred and fifty miles up the road was the camp where his father was imprisoned. 'What for?', we asked. 'For killing my mum. He caught her with another man while he was working in the pits'. 'Did you feel sorry for her?' 'No, he did right'. Those were his very words. He was living with his grandmother and twice a month they would scrape some food together to take to his father at the camp. That boy was a free man. But there were certain things that you couldn't explain to him, and even if

you had tried he wouldn't understand. We could call him a cynic but he wouldn't know the meaning of the word. And he's already beyond its meaning. This is a man without any romantic inclination, but still it's interesting to talk to him.

I once chatted to a guy that earned a bit of money helping on our geological expedition. Out of the blue he asked me what I read. 'Nothing much', I said, 'The French Notebooks'. 'Ah, the Expressionists', he said. Since the age of twelve he's been in different juvenile centres and camps. There were academics there, intellectuals serving time too. He learned a lot from them, he even studied a language but forgot it. I got so interested in him I gave him one of my books. And that was it, I never saw him again. He didn't come to work the next day. A few weeks later he approached my car, he'd completely forgotten about the book, and asked me to buy his camera for ten roubles. The straps were cut. 'For five then', he said, 'enough for a bottle.' If he had had to, he would have killed me and my French Notebooks wouldn't have made any difference. Things like that affect your imagination. For Anna, Osip is an interesting specimen, strong and handsome. He shoots and swims well. There are many things one can envy in him. Strangely enough, it's not Platonov's but Osip's insults that Vengerovich can't bear. (To the actor) You act as if this doesn't affect you at all. But when Osip insults Vengerovich he jumps on Platonov instead. Isn't it interesting why this is so?

Actor: Osip doesn't depend on Vengerovich.

Dodin: Yes, Vengerovich is even a bit afraid of him. He's not afraid of Platonov. Whatever Platonov says, it's just talk. Osip however is a man of action. He is capable of doing many things, and Vengerovich has to pay him for that. There are people that one can't avoid paying. Vengerovich has paid Osip before and not just for maiming Platonov. If he's not paid he might help himself to the money. Osip is on Platonov's side when it comes to Vengerovich. And Vengerovich has to put up with being insulted by a criminal.

Sixteen

Dodin: (Assumes Vengerovich's role): "Please. If I'm to be lectured, it won't be by you. I'm a citizen. A father making a useful contribu-

tion to society. And what are you? A scoundrel, a wastrel, who has squandered his inheritance." (Assumes Platonov's role): "That makes 'citizen' a pretty dirty word." (Assumes Anna's role): "Please, I have already told you. Are you determined to spoil our whole day? Remember, you're a guest." (To the actress) You're offended too. If it wasn't for Platonov things could have taken a different course. When there is a squabble the hosts feel uncomfortable too. (Improvises as Vengerovich): "What have I done to him? The man doesn't give me a break. I need calming down, not him". (Improvises as Platonov): "Why don't you dare speak up? Because we all owe him money. Decency flies out of the window." Platonov is almost in tears. Anna is almost in tears: "That is last year's business. Let's not go over it again."

Platonov takes a glass of water and sits down. Silence.

Shcherbuk I can't begin to tell you how unhappy I am. Better to be six feet under than to live with an unfaithful woman.

Dodin: Shcherbuk, being affected by the agitation, is going into his own emotional melt down. They are all stunned but Shcherbuk's outburst doesn't make things any better. Next – Count Glagolyev *fils* arrives. Now they are really shocked. Imagine a man in a tailcoat showing up in a council flat in the middle of a brawl. This is the awful son that Glagolyev keeps abroad to avoid being shamed, the son that discredits him completely.

Seventeen

Actor: It's rather ironic that Glagolyev lectures about virtue but has a son that he's ashamed of.

Dodin: We can see now that he had his reasons for criticising the younger generation. (To the actor playing Glagolyev) But the son is your responsibility, the generation is nobody's. It's better, when you make the 'old virtues' speech, to have in mind the generation and not the son. With Kyril's arrival the emphasis will shift naturally.

From the very beginning it was a mad, mad day. Everybody was trying to hide something; everybody had an agenda. Kyril's arrival is the last straw. The dirty linen is finally being aired. It's difficult to keep up any decent position in society with a son like that. After

complicating, escalating and entangling to extreme all the lines, just moments before the end of the First Act the seeming balance of power has completely shifted.

It's late and we have to break now. But tomorrow we'll rotate all the roles again because everybody has to be equally engaged.

Day Four

Act One
Seventeen

Dodin: I read Milos Forman's book yesterday. Talking about one of his films he writes about the anti-war movement in the US during the sixties. It struck me that we never had any anti-war movement in this country, neither against the Afghanistan war nor against the war in Chechnya…

How is your dance practice going, are you finding any meaningful moves?

Actor: We just practice different bits.

Dodin: But it's important… You don't have that much time for individual probing so we have to really plan everything carefully. The voice lessons, the music lessons, we'll have to do them in groups at different times. I hope that you understand. People reading certain roles now can test themselves in others. Each of you brings some meaningful touches. We have to explore them all. I think that yesterday we understood what the meeting with Sofya meant to Platonov. As to what it means to Sofya, we understand much less so far. Do you agree with me?

Actress: I do.

Dodin: Do you have some ideas as to what there is there to understand?

Actress: First, the man she was in love with five years ago has changed a lot. She can see this immediately.

Actor: He is substantially changed. But she also went through a major transformation during that time: on Platonov and on her present life. By now she's almost forgotten about him.

Actor: The passage from adolescence to adulthood is accompanied by a substantial hair growth. It's an enormous physical change. Our Platonov is without make up yet. But when he was so young he looked different.

Actress: He was her mentor!

Actor: She remembers him as he was in his youth - how he spoke, how his eyes sparkled.

Dodin: I think these are only partial explanations.

Actor: She exists in a different dimension now. It's difficult even to imagine meeting up with him.

Dodin: The essential thing is not that he has changed on the outside, although he has changed substantially. The important point is that during these years he has become mythical in her mind. Platonov is the most precious thing she had ever had in her life. In her mind he's either in Siberia or has emigrated abroad, because if he had become a minister or something she would have heard about it. I'm sure that when she read the papers she looked for his name. (Improvises as Sofya): "Here they write about a bomb explosion – may be that's him? Or may be he's in Geneva, a party chairman or something." In Sofya's mind Platonov is somewhere else, in another country, in another dimension. And they won't ever meet again. They went their different ways, their paths parted. Despite that Sofya recognises him almost immediately. But it's very difficult for her to connect the man that she knew, that image she'd created in her mind with the present figure. She can't understand - something that feels so intimate, so close in a figure so alien and different... Different not in the way he's dressed although he's the most poorly dressed of them all.

Actor: How can she talk to him now, which words should she use?

Dodin: The depth of Sofya's shock is enormous – she sees what life can do to people, how it can destroy their dreams. The relationship with Platonov was the most meaningful part of her life...

I knew the wonderful Russian writer Vasili Belov for years. Then I read some abominable thing he wrote in the papers. It wasn't just disappointment in Belov as a writer; it's much more than that. A part of my previous life was turned upside down and was gone. The best part.

Actor: It's not clear to me how they parted - what happened and why.

Dodin: It's a good question but you have to find the answer yourself.

Actor: Women were not allowed to go to university then, to do a full degree. The struggle for emancipation was just starting. A lot of women went on to continue their studies beyond high school. The universities set up some courses for them. Sofya Perovskaya and Sofya Kovalevskaya were Sofya's contemporaries. Platonov could have been her lecturer on one of these courses. He was reading philology and he could have taken one of the women's courses. That's how they could have met. Or may be they met at some debating society gathering. It was the time of the first political demonstrations in Russia. They could have mixed in the same circles and then parted when he left university. But why did he leave university? May be he had to leave because of his father's death, or because he got so bored with all the talking that he decided to go and do something more useful instead. Perhaps he decided to go back to the people. And what kind of relationship did they have? Was it love? 'The girl loved the student, the student loved the girl', she says. (Act Two, Scene One, Six) Yes, it was love. But then how did he break up the whole thing? And why did he leave university? I don't think that he became a schoolmaster out of idealistic conviction.

Actor: Leaving everything must have given him even stronger romantic flair.

Actress: He didn't have any money for a long time before his father's death. His father died three years ago and Platonov had ceased getting any money from him three years before that.

Dodin: When he got his hands on some, he would spend it: he would buy out one prostitute after another. We mustn't overstate his revolutionary activities: mostly that's what they were.

Actor: In Chekhov's *Duel* the character's first lover was a widow. Then he decided to buy out a prostitute, to 'bring her up to his level'. The prostitute stayed with him for a while and then ran back to her Madam.

Dodin: (Improvises as Platonov): "Sofie, Mimi, Masha... there are so many of you... I love you all... I went to university... I demon-

strated at the Theatre Square... I bought out Raisa... we had a collection with some other students and bought out another one... I have her letters..."

We still tend to idealise the people that took part in some revolutionary activity or another. We still have this Soviet thing that the best people were the ones who took part in the revolution. Today we have a more sober view on those who go into politics or into terrorism... Firstly, the ones that are good at studying don't go into terrorism, with minor exceptions. Triletsky's mentioning that the two of them were not the best at overcoming their carnal desires or that they didn't fail their Latin by accident. (Act Two, Scene One, Eleven)

It's much easier and more fun to engage with loftier issues and take part in important movements. Of course there were people with grand characters like Sofya Perovskaya who worked to challenge the concept of the family; there were ideas of emancipation, free love and civic marriage. But often it was the energy of youth or vanity that drove young people to the squares and propelled them into demonstrations. And there is nothing wrong with that. Sometimes it's easier to join the crowds than enter a theatre. Platonov spent quite a lot of money and time on things that got him noticed and made him special in people's eyes. Only a small part of his energy was spent on his studies even though he was capable. He picked up ideas on the way between demonstrations and debating societies - that was his education. As for Sofya, what do you thing was her story? How did the break up affect her?

Actor: In my view they didn't meet in the city. He used to come to the country in the summer. She was a high school girl and they met in the village, at the estate. They spent their holidays together and met everyday. Of course, she was very much taken by him, young, talented and good looking.

Actor: Question: Did Sofya know that she was coming to the same region which she used to visit on holiday or does the realisation only come after they mention Platonovka. The places were named after the estate: she might not have known that Voynitzevka is close to Platonovka.

Dodin: (Assumes Sofya's role): "Platonovka? It still exists? I once

knew its owner."

Actress: On her way there did she know that Sergei Voynitzev was Platonov's friend? She might not have known that Platonov was back and living there but maybe she knew that this was where he was born?

Actor: They could have been at university together, with Platonov being a year or two ahead of her.

Dodin: I think the idea that they met somewhere in the country side, where Platonov was the only guy from Saint Petersburg, is a good one. He opened her eyes on how life should be. He simply woke her for life. It wasn't an ordinary friendship between two young people. She hadn't yet been a student back then. But after finishing school she did all she could to get to Saint Petersburg and go to university. When she finally arrived he was no longer there. Instead of Platonov she found Voynitzev, which came rather handy. Of course, they would have never discussed Platonov. It's a different story though that Sergei is a very similar guy, same fancies, same passions. Of course not of the same level but still, from the crowd that surrounded her, Voynitzev wouldn't have been the worst.

Actor: It's very difficult to beat your first teacher, the person that opened your eyes to life. It leaves the finest and brightest of memories.

Dodin: Young Platonov with the delightful Sofya next to him: their pairing looks very much like the one he has now with Maria Grekova. But he's a different man and with Maria is more like a parody of what he had with Sofya. Maria went a step further - she went to read chemistry. Sofya took only her first lessons in life from him. And then he simply left. The holiday ended. Life threw him here and there, he got caught up by things and he just disappeared...

I think she knew that they were coming into this area but she had no way of knowing that Platonov had come back to live in the village of his birth. Still the thought of where he was and what might have happened to him had never left her. (Improvises as Sofya): "I love my Sergei, I married him, but that – that was a different life." Sofya has achieved a lot: she made it to Saint Petersburg, she finished her course. She's ready to act. She's full of a young woman's energy that's fuelling her desire to do things. Repin has this marvellous por-

trait – you can see a young lass just bursting with energy. And the only thing there was there to spend this energy on was love. Don't we say: new love – new life. We still believe it but nowadays there are other considerations - career, travel, fitness, charity, plenty of things. Back then there was only love.

This version of their story also allows for that romantic touch that you talked about. I think that Platonov's disappearance has coloured everybody's perception of him in romantic tones. The dissident has disappeared – it surely means that he's sent to Siberia. (To the actress) It fits, doesn't it?

Actress: It makes me feel sorry.

Dodin: For whom?

Actress: Initially Platonov just disappoints you but then my woman's heart starts feeling sorry for him.

Dodin: I'm not sure that we should.

Actor: More likely Sofya would think, 'What has become of me?' It's self-pity, she's sorry for herself more than anything else.

Dodin: You can see how much has happened on this first day of her stay; how many things are heaped on her head. It's not accidental that on the way to the dinner table Platonov takes her on his arm. (Improvises as Platonov): "You see, my darling, the state of affairs. Mortified, is that why your jaw has dropped? Mortified of the world you came into? Yes, that's the world of fools, traitors, crooks, midgets…"

Platonov offers Sofya his arm.

Platonov   Yes. It's as bad as you think it is. A world made up only of the utterly third-rate. That's who we are. That's what we are. What beautiful eyes you have.

Platonov smiles at her as they go to lunch.

Dodin: They're again the teacher and the acolyte, can you see it?

Actor: Of course, Platonov's becoming again her teacher in life. (Improvises as Platonov): "Theory is one thing, it's a different story to live for a while and learn from practice how real life is.

Dodin: To Platonov she's like a stubborn splinter that he can't get out. (Improvises as Platonov): "You see, my darling, you stare at me in surprise but see what you have got yourself into. Look what life

does to people…" He doesn't come near her, clutch her hand, follow her about, stare at her, as she claims. (Act Two, Scene One, Six). He just goes on to explain to her how life has dealt with her, with everybody, with all of them. He tries to make them both feel united in their disgrace but doesn't make any excuse for himself. (Improvises as Platonov): "Here I am, living somehow, out of place, but what's the point of talking of me. It's all clear: I'm finished, gone, but you-u-u! You-u-u! This is the climax of his plea to her. "How could you do it? Why didn't you choose someone else? How could you give yourself to this nonentity? This pygmy? This loafer? Why couldn't you find someone decent, a labourer, a worker, an employee, someone that is capable of doing something. You don't have to answer, just don't tell me you're offended! You can't be offended for his sake. You can't love him, because there is nothing about him to love!" (Improvises as Sofya): "How dare you tell me all this? What shall I do now? Of course you're right? What a disaster!"

In some way Platonov really is right. He will later say: "I'm unworthy, I'm ashamed." (Act Two, Scene Two, Three). "What wrong did her husband ever do to me? But there I stood, peddling my usual theatrical bilge." (Act Two, Scene Two, Four). But these self-accusations make him immediately look like the best in this crowd, the only one.

Sofya, on the other hand, is alarmed by the fact that very quickly he is resuming the place he once had in her affections. This frustration will grow fast and explode in Act Two. (Assumes Sofya's role): "I started to find you unbearable…What right do you have to come near me… as if the past gave you a licence. And to what end? What's the point of this pursuit? Where do you wish it to lead?" (Act Two, Scene One, Six). (Improvises as Platonov): "You're scared. God, I can't believe this! Simply telling the truth makes her think that I want her! I can't believe you've fallen so low."

Actress: He can talk only to her about these things.

Dodin: Not really, in one way or another he's been sharing his thoughts or views with everybody.

Actor: He later rejects Anna too and he's very earnest about it.

Dodin: What do you mean 'reject'?

Actor: She offered herself and he declined.

Dodin: Not exactly. He was ready to do it. If it wasn't for Sasha, it would have happened. Why do you think he didn't do it?

Actor: Anna asks him: "I don't understand. You must be going mad. Here we are, we're in love with each other. What more do you want?" (Act Three, Five).

Actor: Sasha is constantly on his mind. He later says to her: "I know I have wronged you, I'm Sofya's lover, possibly Anna's lover, too" – that isn't quite clear yet – "I haven't always lived up to my own standards, I know that. But nobody's going to love you as I do."

Dodin: Why doesn't he take Anna?

Actor: I think there are certain issues that bother him. He can't forget about them. First of all, there is Glagolyev. Platonov knows about his intentions.

Dodin: What you are talking about is a different question - the question of the general complexity of the relationships there. But now we are discussing Platonov's and Anna's affair; we have to keep to the facts. You said that Platonov rejects her but I don't see it that way. I seems to me that nobody's rejecting anyone; the romance is very much developing.

Actor: But he's very firm about…

Dodin: About what?

Actor: Is he lying when he says that he'll call by in the evening.

Dodin: I don't think he's lying. No.

Actor: But in Act Two…

Dodin: In Act Two, I think that they planned everything exactly in Act Two.

Actor: Why he says 'possibly Anna's lover, too', why 'possibly'?

Actress: Because nothing has happened yet.

Dodin: I see it the other way round, 'possibly', because practically they've already decided that they will elope together. Let's read this carefully: (assumes Platonov's role): "May be I should have a word with Sofya. Ask her outright: how about delaying? Not for long, just a couple of weeks, and then I could go somewhere with Anna. Sofya can go to her mother's, she'd like that… And she needs a rest, God knows, from the look of her. It could work." Next thing Anna is knocking at the door. I think it's clear that Anna and Platonov had alrea-

dy talked it over at some point – where and when exactly they did is a different story. Because things never happen like that: 'Shall we?' – 'Yes!' – 'Let's go!'. This can't be. It can – only in Charing Cross' red district. People prepare for something like that, at least mentally.

Actor: Then how could Anna have overlooked Platonov's romance with Sofya for so long?

Dodin: Why do you thing that she missed it?

Actor: Because she learns about it only in Act Four, when Voynitzev says to her: "Sofya is not mine and Platonov's not yours."

Dodin: I remember everything that she says, but I think that until the very last moment she tries to avoid thinking of this - she's in denial. She's not blind. She sees what's happening with Sofya, she sees what's happening with Sergei. It's another matter that she can't accept it until the very end and, perhaps, she doesn't want to. Everybody sees everything. It turns out Sofya knows everything about Anna. At the end she'll say to her: "And you! You turned him against me. It was you that did it. You're worse than he is. You're worse." (Act Four, Eight). It's only from the outside that it looks as if no one knows anything.

Think of some personal situations that you seemingly didn't know about at first: you didn't know in the beginning, then after a day or two, you start to get an inkling, to overhear things and certain thoughts occur to you. Anna came to Platonov because she felt there was something; she realised what it was and she wanted to change it. That's how I think it was.

Actor: I still don't understand about Anna…

Dodin: You won't understand it now. We have to read it through, read all the episodes. You got stuck with this impression of Platonov's reaction towards Anna: "I'll kill myself if I stay here"; "In the name of God, in God's own name, will you please help me? Will you please go?"; "Please go, because if you don't then I'll know I shall just want to kill myself." And so on. This is a completely different love from the one he has for Sofya. Different relationship, different romance, different story. Do you understand what I mean?

Actor: She's a different woman.

Dodin: That too. Different woman, different deal. She has other ne-

eds, offers other challenges, excites other sides of his being. That's why the thought that after all he could continue with both affairs came to his mind. With one of them he has to start a whole new life and that's impossible; with the other he just has to continue his life and that's more practical. But let's go back to the end of Act One where we left them.

Platonov   A world made up only of the utterly third-rate. That's who we are. That's what we are.

Dodin: (Improvises as Platonov): "And you, Sofya, you are part of this now and forever. You're a true and compulsory member of this crowd. That's the place where you found yourself, Sofya Yegorovna. After five years of this life you will be unrecognisable too; the first woman to finish Bestuzhev's course will be gone... That's the life you've chosen for yourself..." And Platonov's monologue goes on and on... If we jump forward we'll see how Sofya's monologue grows out of his. (Assumes Sofia's role): "My husbands lips move, but they make no sound. For days on end I no longer think of him... Platonov shows me no mercy. Everywhere I go he pursues me. And I know... just the sight of him, the smell of him. I know: just one step and I'm lost." (Act Two, Scene One, Five).

That's it: it started immediately, from their very first meeting. (Assumes Platonov's role): "You can't control character. Man's character is fiery, but lack of fire is even worse." (Act One, Twenty). That's what exploded into an elemental storm with the arrival of Sofya.

Actor: I wonder if Triletsky also fell in love with Sofya from the very first moment she came in?

Dodin: Of course, he was deeply impressed by her although she barely noticed him. That's why Triletsky's affection is a bit defensive. Very often being hurt is the strongest reason to fall in love. Why does Triletsky goes on disparaging her all the time? (Assumes Triletsky's role): "She thinks she has only to open her mouth, to offer her world-shattering insights and the whole of Russia will come running to sit at her feet. And her contempt!...For me. For you. As if her precious Sergei were in any way better than us." (Improvises as Triletsky): "She doesn't pay any attention to me but at least I'm a doctor. What is he?"

Actor: But also Triletsky saw Sofya at the worst possible moment for him - when he had just been publicly humiliated by Maria's outburst. Then he had to run after her in the garden to calm her down. He rushed back pretty agitated and there was Sofya: of course she impressed him deeply.

Eighteen

Petrin   Are you going to marry her?
Porfiri   I haven't asked her.
Petrin   But you think there's a chance?

Dodin: Glagolyev and Petrin's exchange is funny. (To the actor playing Glagolyev) I don't think you would be confiding in him. It's unlikely that Glagolyev will confide or seek advice from anybody. Petrin's simply clings to you, like a leech. (Improvises as Glagolyev): "I don't know… I never asked her… how can I say…" (Back to the actor again) You don't have to discuss this with anybody. You do your own thing; you follow your own direction. And after all, why would you discuss it with Petrin, he's a scoundrel.

Actor: Then I can immediately show him his place.

Dodin: That's what you do in fact. But you can't really show him the finger. You do it by showing dominance.

Actor: Glagolyev's not recovered yet from the unexpected meeting with his son…

Dodin: There are all sorts of things that he hasn't recovered from yet. He's taking on a serious challenge with Anna, and suddenly so many things have piled up. (To the actor playing Glagolyev) Platonov insults you. (Assumes Glagolyev's role): "Please, this is no longer funny!" Petrin annoys and humiliates you. (Improvises as Petrin): "The woman owes me, for God's sake. A marriage isn't just between two people. If she marries Porfiri, then I get my money back." Note the remark and then play it.

Porfiri goes out. Petrin is left alone.

Nineteen

Petrin   Anna, I can paper the walls with your IOUs.

Anna   You only have IOUs because you wangled them out of the General when he was dying. Dying and drunk, I may say.

Dodin: Very good. Why am I trying to follow Petrin's entire line through? Because I want you to feel and understand that this is one uninterrupted line all the way through. We can't play it: he said – she said, I asked – she answered, if she didn't – I wouldn't. (Improvises as Petrin): "I live in poverty but have vouchers for sixteen thousand in my pocket... I wonder, dear Anna, could I just make a small suggestion?" (Assumes Anna's role): "That's not exactly a 'suggestion'. How much you need? A rouble? Two?"

Obviously this is a never ending argument between them, it has become part of their lives. He nags and nags and she consistently turns him down again and again. This little battle of theirs takes quite some resilience and stamina. And preferably it mustn't be conducted in front of other people. Some decorum has to be sustained. Anna's so frustrated with this ongoing onslaught that, lost for arguments, she launches into nonsense. (Reading Anna's line): "Why should I pay you back? It's a waste. You're going to be dead very soon. Doesn't that ever occur to you? What's the point of this bullying? Sue if you like, it doesn't bother me at all."

Petrin threatens, begs, cries, drivels but he's always there in the background. It doesn't matter how little attention she pays to him, this constant pressure must be quite unnerving. She has to play the game of 'push and pull', and keep him under control. (To the actress) We have to find a way to express this double play.

Petrin   Who was the General's best friend? Who closed his eyes when he died?

Anna   You, Petrin. You. You. And much good may it do you.

Petrin   You should be careful, Anna. You're proud and arrogant. Pride is a sin.

Dodin: Petrin exits only because Platonov comes in. It's not over. They just slip away from each other to find another moment when nobody's there to renew the sparring. They inhabit the same stable so to speak. If only Anna could scratch their eyes out, she would, but the *bon ton* has to be sustained at all costs. Petrin looks like a second

class player but his line is very important for the density of the overall picture.

Twenty

Platonov   Let me kiss your hand. *(Platonov kneels and kisses her hand.)* Throw them out. Throw them all out.

Dodin: Let's recap. Platonov was obnoxious and arrogant; he caused a heated argument, interrupted by Kiril Glagolyev's unexpected arrival. Then hunger has drawn them away from the veranda to the table laid for lunch. Platonov's wants to soothe the impression and apologise. (Assumes Platonov's role): "I'm sorry. I got carried away." But of course he's not sorry. And he hasn't calmed down. (Improvises as Platonov): "How can I calm down. I do things that I shouldn't do. I'm torn between affection and regret. You're the last person I want to cross, let's be friends again. But they're all garbage… they deserve to be kicked out of the door… As long as they're here I can't calm down… but I can see you're getting angry with me again…".

Actress: This is their moment, isn't it? It's very private. She pours out all the pain she feels. To Platonov.

Anna   How can we be decent when we're in debt? One word against these people and they can cut me off and leave me for dead. I owe them all money, every one of them. Oh yes, decency's a fine thing. But if I have to choose between decency and losing the estate… *(Anna looks at him a moment.)* Don't talk to me about decency. And don't interfere… You and I, we'll go riding this afternoon. *(Anna puts her hand on his shoulder.)*

Dodin: Platonov's last line after Anna moves towards the table is the most interesting one. (Assumes Platonov's role): "But why should these people be allowed to behave as they do?" (Improvises as Platonov): They'll see! I'll show them! And I'll show Sofya too! I promised myself not to touch this dirt ever again: promised a long time ago and for the second time this morning. But what can I do? I can't control myself… Man's character is fiery but being placid is even worse…"

Twenty One

Isaac   I've come to give the school master a piece of advice.…
I think you should leave my father alone.

Dodin: Whenever they happen to be next to each other, Isaac attacks
Platonov head on: he's a strong opponent. Platonov says about him:
"My, what a big-hearted boy you are. The idealist, the man of principle." Actually, Vengerovich *fils* is close to the truth when he says that
the reason Platonov provokes his father and everybody else is nothing
more than boredom. 'You think you're pursuing truth, but you're not,'
he says to Platonov. What you're chasing is entertainment.' And later,
'You don't pick a quarrel with my father in private. No, always in front
of an audience.' If we listen to the insults they throw at each other – it's
pretty heavy stuff: (alternately improvises as Isaac and Platonov) "Leave my father alone"… "Tell him from me to drop dead"… "what you
do, it isn't a moral crusade, it's theatre"… "I'd love to see you in ten years"… "Better to be alive, better true feelings for ten minutes than live
with false feelings for ten years". It's a full blown brawl. By today's
standards it's a real fisticuffs, they're bashing each other's brains
out. In those days they had duels to sort out such arguments. But
Platonov would never challenge a Jew to a duel.

This is a very physical confrontation. We can see from the remarks
that during the exchange they point at each other, turn their back to
walk away then turn back in indignation…

Actor: It's one scandal after another. They don't stop moving…

Dodin: Of course.

Actor: It's a pile of egos and obsessions cramped in a tight space.
There might be some nudging and poking, clenching of fists and
knuckle cracking going on, but still, it's the salon of Anna Petrovna.

Dodin: It's not a 'salon'. And there's no need to think of it that way.
Let's not stray from the core of things.

Actress: So many awful confrontations and bad things have happened in this house!

Dodin: But they didn't fall from the sky. Anna didn't come here to
throw dinner parties; she came to cut deals, so deals are being cut… If
somebody from outside comes to our rehearsal room they might think

'oh how interesting'! But I know that rehearsals are a tough thing: if something doesn't work there would be shouting, somebody might cry, we'd be tearing our hair out and God knows to what end. But I know that that's what rehearsal is like and I live with it. That's life.

Actress: Still, (improvises as Anna) I have invited guests for lunch...

Dodin: You didn't invite guests. Who's invited here? Is Vengerovich invited? They all came to visit her.

Actor: Even Osip came with an excuse, to congratulate her for her birthday and Sergei for his wedding.

Actress: (Improvises as Anna): "I know that these are all important people."

Dodin: Important? How? If it was up to her she wouldn't have met Vengerovich for ages, but now this is his house. (Improvises as Anna): "I wouldn't have missed Petrin either but I can't throw him out because the next day he'd go spreading vile rumours about me..." They are not guests and this is not a ball!

Actress: But later there will be a celebration.

Dodin: That's right. She has to keep good relationships with all these people. (Improvises as Anna): "If I didn't have to be obliging I would've let them go straight to hell." Why do people bother throwing parties, giving receptions and so on? Because it's good for business, not for pleasure.

Actress: What about all these scandals and quarrels, are they normal?

Dodin: What's normal?

Actress: So it's all one total mess, things going dreadfully wrong, nothing ending as expected...

Dodin: To me this is an abstract conversation that we don't need to go into. What happens, happens. What has a 'salon' or 'dinner party' got to do with it? That's why we sit here and dissect the play, scrutinising every word: to get to understand that it's not a 'salon' and it's not a 'dinner party' and Anna's not some high class socialite. We have to destroy all those preconceptions. We have to get to the core of every single move: why he or she does or says this and not that at this or that particular moment. That's what we are interested in - the facts. Not the style, code or decorum, whatever they mean, if anything.

Actor: The lunch is paid for with Vengerovich's money.

Dopdin: Of course. Where would she find money to feed them? It's all been borrowed.

Actor: Why don't they borrow from Glagolyev?

Actor: Glagolyev has lent them enough already.

Dodin: They might be taking from Bugrov too, but everybody knows that Bugrov himself lives on Vengerovich's money. They are all neighbours. Their estates are adjacent. They are all connected. It's like a communal flat. It's a different matter that they keep their chins up and can say a few words in French: they may know only a few words but can speak them without an accent because they were all taught by French governesses when they were young. But a county district is in essence a communal flat with all the chatter and clutter.

Twenty Two

Dodin: This is the last scene of the First Act. By now we've seen the whole gallery of characters strolling by. Stories, loves, secrets, aspirations have all been thrown into the pot. Old and new passions mixed, new interests threatened, and there it is, a time bomb set to be released over the next acts.

This is an important scene because after all the innuendoes Sergei spells out the deal with Glagolyev. All the cards are on the table waiting to be played.

Platonov   I've been looking at your wife, Sergei. You're a fortunate man… She's still beautiful but once she was even more beautiful.

Dodin: It's quite an outburst, to say such a thing to a husband. (Improvises as Platonov): "I've known her longer than you. I know her like the back of my hand."

Sergei   More? I don't believe you.

Platonov   It's true. Her eyes.

Sergei   Her hair.

Dodin: A strange situation. Two men discussing the charms of… the Mona Lisa or something. Then he begins immediately to talk about Sasha, his wife: (assumes Platonov's role) "And what about my

own wife? There she is perspiring and flustered, hidden behind the vodka bottle. Her blunt, peasant features blushing red. In agony, as always, over my behaviour." (Improvises as Platonov's role): "I can see she's suffering… poor soul! And she's mine, nobody else's…" In other words that is his life. This part of their conversation should be as bold and heightened as the one about Sofya.

Sergei   Forgive me, but, tell me, are you happy with your wife?

Platonov   She's my wife. That's what she is. Without her, I'm lost. One day you'll understand family. How important family is.

Dodin: This is a serious conversation. They are now truly earnest with each other; talking about big stuff. Voynitzev has yet to understand what family is. It's a very strong thing to say, 'without her, I'm lost'. Sasha is Platonov's only anchor holding him to this world. Without her he'd have become a drunkard a long time ago. (Assumes Platonov's role): "I wouldn't sell Sasha for a million roubles." Voynitzev still doesn't understand because this doesn't answer his question - is Platonov happy? 'She's stupid and I'm worthless. In other words, we're perfectly matched', Platonov says.

The relationship between Sasha and Platonov is a very serious one. He never ever betrays her. Some of his actions do, but he never betrays in his heart. (Improvises as Platonov): "Once she was even more beautiful! And my life… it's like a different galaxy… it's not that the one is beautiful and the other's ugly. It's simply millions of light years away… which one I need more I don't know." Platonov and Sasha love each other. And generally, I believe that Platonov had only one true love in his life and that was Sasha. No one would have ever thought it to be true, and may be that's why Platonov's embarrassed to admit it openly. All his other infatuations, with Anna, with Sofya, they're easy to understand, but this one… He's hoping that his friend Sergei will understand.

Nikolai comes back, slapping his stomach with satisfaction.

Nikolai   Solid as a rock. This is the life. Come on, a little drink everyone.

Dodin: Triletsky has an instinct for conflict. (To the actor) You know what conflict is, don't you? If it's there, it's there all the time; it doesn't go away no matter what.

Actor: Did Anna send Triletsky to call Platonov to the table?

Dodin: No, I think he had a bite hastily and left the table.

Actor: Pretending he can't stand the company any longer...

Dodin: And Triletsky did too. But Triletsky was really hungry. And it's not every day that they lay a table like that. All his exclamations and gestures show he had the meal of his life.

Platonov   Just asking, but have you actually visited a single patient today?

Dodin: (Improvises as Platonov): "You've completely lost your head, you came running here in the morning, waited ages for that lunch and forgot about everything..."

Again, to a certain extent Platonov is saying this about himself, he too has forgotten about everything. Triletsky doesn't want to talk about this, he says, 'we'll talk about this later'. What does 'later' mean? It means that his patients are waiting. This is not small talk. They are real patients; they exist. I happened to talk to a doctor the other day – Triletsky in the flesh. Unfortunately, there are so many of them around. Big guy, moustache, looked a bit like Chekhov from his early pictures. He promised he would do this and that, but did nothing. You know our hospitals, you bring in somebody in pain and if you're lucky enough to see a doctor, they take a look, excuse themselves for a second and then disappear. You get the impression they are so busy somewhere else that they can't come down to the ward. And seriously sick people are just lying there. Everything that can be snatched is gone, even the window handles are gone; old papers are stuffed between the frames. What do they do in winter? It's unbelievable. But just try telling them they're bad doctors! They are not so bad actually, sometimes they can help. It's called 'Clinical Centre for Advanced Medical Technologies'! There is no running water for weeks; no hot water, just cold water. It's switched off. And this is the main hospital of the city.

(Improvises as Triletsky): "Now you've spoiled my good mood! Leave me alone, I'm fed up with your lectures! I'm fed up with you!" It's a strong reaction and the interesting thing is that the outburst comes out of nowhere. Platonov hasn't touched on this subject for a long time. It's just a joke. It means that this conflict has been brewing for

some time.

Nikolai Any criticisms you have, put them in writing. Better still, set an hour aside everyday for you to detail my imperfections. Four till five, Platonov's preaching.

Dodin: It means that Triletsky has hidden his feelings for a long time, that he felt deeply that Platonov's insults were unjust. When does somebody start talking too much? While Triletsky is talking, Platonov's obviously looking at him in a certain way. See the remark.

Platonov frowns, looking at Sergei.

Dodin: We have a very interesting sequence here: Platonov only says a few words, then he waits patiently for Triletsky to finish and turns not to him but to Voynitzev: "One thing I did wonder… That advertisement in today's paper." He didn't even react to Triletsky's tirade. (Assumes Platonov's role): "An auction? Are things really so bad?"

This is one of the main questions that has brought Platonov here today. It's the opening situation of the entire play – the estate going up for auction. Their private lives are just decorations on the canvas of a totally different picture. That's why they are all here: the estate will leave one person's hands and move to the hands of another; somebody will lose, somebody will gain and so on and so on… If the Voynitzev family are impoverished Petrin gets nothing. He needs Glagolyev to marry Anna. They are all dragged here by the situation with the estate. It has to be evaluated, change ownership, a new owner has to take control etc. The bountiful lunch is a treat for the creditors, a settling of accounts with them which has to be postponed until the planned deal with Glagolyev is closed.

At the end the whole operation falls through in the same way that everything else falls through. In essence, whichever way you look at it, Anna, with the help of Glagolyev, has planned a financial affair that blows up in their faces. And of course Sergei also has taken part in the details of the deal no matter how much he pretends that he didn't. Glagolyev is Anna's senior partner but other people are dragged in too. Shcherbuk is promptly despatched by his wife to take care of his lot; he also pretends he's not involved. (Improvises as Shcherbuk): "I'm just popping by to say hello, to greet you on the occasion, that's all… I don't ask for anything…I'm just a friend…"

Although he rushed here for only one reason - to protect his interest.

Actor: Is Glagolyev *fils* involved also?

Dodin: I'm not sure.

Actor: I don't think that in the Act One he knew about the scheme.

Dodin: Later he noticed that he's not been sent his allowance, that the money's been invested somewhere else. Everything has been wasted on this whore, you see, he's deprived, can't take advantage of the whore either, it's not fair... I think that he simply fell out of the tree, as they say, but landed on just the right spot.

Actor: If his father marries he will lose his inheritance.

Actor: And that's his only chance.

Actress: If Glagolyev has the money, why can't they sell the estate straight to him?

Actor: Because it has been already re-mortgaged. At the auction Vengerovich can bid higher and everything will collapse. So Glagolyev publishes the article in the paper to scare him off.

Dodin: Glagolyev simply wants to play it safe. He's already bought out one lot, he'll buy this one too. It's competition.

Actor: Bugrov will then come with the vouchers he'd bought out from the General. Does Glagolyev know about that?

Dodin: He knows. That's what the competition is about. He's taking a risk. That's how he won Anna over, with his ability to take risks.

Actress: Why would the Voynitzevs take the risk? Can't they live quietly, pay the interest?

Dodin: They have nothing to pay it with. (Improvises as Anna): "We boxed ourselves into a corner. If only we had lived quietly, paid the interest, we could have wriggled out somehow..." She decides to go ahead with the sale when she can't get any interest or they can't both live on it.

Actress: Why can't Glagolyev buy out the estate or give her money to buy it out herself?

Dodin: How can one give money to a woman? And how can she take it?

Actor: Why does he need to buy the estate at all?

Dodin: When they die the estate becomes his. It's as if I'm offering

you: I'll buy a flat; I don't need it now, you live in it; I'll still own the property, it's my collateral. You just have to say thank you. He's done his maths very carefully. (Improvises as Glagolyev): "I'll take care of all your problems with the estate." Of course, with this generous offer he's tied Anna's hands. She understands this very well but she has to play the part. She simply hopes that she'll find some way to wriggle out later. She even says at some point, 'To be honest, I don't know why you need me.' (Act Two, Scene One, Fourteen).

Actor: Does this mean that she didn't encourage him? But the idea of marrying her couldn't have come to him out of nowhere, just because he's a romantic? He's pragmatic, which means that she must have encouraged him somehow, with her behaviour or attitude.

Dodin: What do you mean 'encouragement'? There were no kisses, there were no hugs, were there?

Actor: She's very flattering towards him.

Dodin: I don't think so.

Actor: He gets more attention than anybody else.

Dodin: Yes, he's round the house from early morning; he's allowed to lecture her stepson as if he were part of the family.

Actress: Glagolyev doesn't buy the estate out of romantic feelings; it's the sensible thing to do.

Dodin: I think the greatest encouragement was to allow him to help her after knowing about his feelings. He's not hiding his feelings but he's also not expecting her to respond. He offers to buy out the estate and to become her patron and protector. He offers to marry her, 'but is happy to forego conjugal rights'. (Act Two, Scene One, Fourteen). He has everything; he's built his earthly paradise; he just needs someone to share it with. Her foreplay is mostly in that she allows him to make all the advances. She accepted the offer; she accepted the letter with his proposal; she didn't expressly say 'no'. Who knows, the third time of asking she might even say 'yes'. Then they would see how exactly to sort out the business side of it later. That's life; things change. That's what he's thinking

Actor: She has promised to think about the letter. This is already a lot.

Dodin: He's completely honest. (Improvises as Glagolyev): "I want

to protect you. It's my pleasure to feel I am of some use to you. Is there something wrong in that? You can have at your disposal everything that belongs to me. But I can't do this for a woman with whom I have no legal status. At least officially she has to be my wife. As God's my witness, if you prefer things to stay as they are between us, I'm ready to forego my conjugal rights. I simply want to do this for you, as a man who's in love. If you love somebody else, I will accept that too. It would be enough for me to know that you're next to me. I mean it sincerely... perhaps part of me believes that you can win someone's love once the other man has shown himself unworthy, by being there the shoulder to cry on. People can think what they want but I'm honest, I'm fighting for my love and that's a romantic thing to do, isn't it?

Actor: Glagolyev wins whichever way things go. If he buys the estate she'll become dependent on him. If Vengerovich buys it, she won't have any protection and will depend on him all the same.

Dodin: It's true, but I don't think we have to burden Glagolyev with such a calculating mind.

Actor: Vengerovich's interest in the estate is purely business, which means he won't pay more than its worth. Glagolyev's position in this sense is much stronger.

Dodin: Glagolyev is prepared to pay more because he's paying for her too. But it seems to me that they don't have vile intentions. And that's a very important thing for us to understand. They do bad thing but are not motivated by bad intentions. Infatuations and obsessions rule their actions more than anything else. Glagolyev is truly, passionately in love. But it's somehow unfair that from the outside it all looks ridiculous or insincere or odd. From the outside everything can look ridiculous or odd, even love itself.

As for Anna, she has somehow to break through this dilemma. She says later: "I'll tell you... what it's like being me. And how there's no hell on earth worse than being an educated woman. You see, people need a dog, they need a cow... You know what to do with them. But I'm not needed... I need a rest." (Act Three, Five).

Let's go back to Platonov's all important line at the end of Act One.

Platonov   That advertisement today in the paper... An auction?

Are things really that bad?

Dodin: What he means by asking this is much deeper. It's not just 'are things bad?' He's asking, 'has it finally happened?' It's been hanging over their heads, it had to happen and it is happening: certain people, a certain class are losing their property and status. It's a historical inevitability.

Sergei I don't think they're bad. As I understand, it's some sort of commercial fiddle, that's all.

Dodin: Voynitzev obviously tries to undermine the seriousness of the situation. He's hiding something. Platonov is not convinced; he's waiting for an explanation. The dots show that there is a pause here. Let's look at Platonov's line after Voynitzev goes into great lengths to explain the details of the deal.

Platonov Why's he doing it? It's hardly out of the goodness of his heart? What's in it for him?

Dodin: (To the actor) Very good. You can hear the offence in his voice. (Improvises as Platonov): "If it's a gift, it's demeaning. But it's not a gift. It's a down payment. That's what people call it." Voynitzev has heard this. He rattles on about the 'blasted bank', about 'the interest or something' they'll pay to Glagolyev and then abruptly changes the subject.

Sergei No more business. Come on, let's all drink and be friends... As long as we're living and Sofya's living and Anna Petrovna's living...that's what matters. Come, let's drink to them all.

Dodin: It's a moan, it's such a cry from the heart. This is obviously a man who's been badly hit. Platonov's words truly got to him. In essence it's a similar monologue to Triletsky's one. They've both been deeply hurt by different things.

It's no accident that Act One ends here. This is the main conversation of the Act. Everything has been turning around this. (Improvises as Triletsky): "I hate the bank. Let's drink to you, my friends! I don't give a damn if fate takes everything away from me! Let the world go to hell!" He truly feels that everything's been taken away from him. It's despair; it's life on the brink, on the edge of an abyss.

Platonov can empathise with what Voynitzev is saying. 'I haven't been drunk for so long', he 'says. Shall we get drunk?' Another one

bites the dust.

Anna   Oh, just look at them! The three of them. *(Sings)* 'Find me a harness for my three horses…'

Dodin: 'Troika' friendship! What an old-fashioned idea from the distant past. We are in the Twentieth century now! That's the association she's making. (Improvises as Anna): "But still this is our 'troika'; at least as good as we get them around here…"

Nikolai *(sings)* 'My horses gallop in a troika'. Let's start on the cognac, why not?

Anna   Come on and eat your lunch, you lazy parasites.

Dodin: A disappearing clan, a species on the path to extinction, that's what they are. They are all parasites. You see, they all live on charity, they're all spongers, except perhaps Platonov. (Improvises as Anna addressing Platonov): "If only I could be with you for ever, if only I could start my life anew…"

At this point here Anna is close to tears and Triletsky's close to tears too. Because it has just become clear to them that the Voynitzevs have nothing. Triletsky wasn't sure; he suspected it but could never bring himself to ask. At this point everything becomes very clear. At the very beginning of the play he tried to ask Anna. Now the realisation has finally dawned on them all. The answer to the question that started all this has revealed itself. This family is perishing. Here we can see the future *Cherry Orchard*. It is one and the same theme: Chekhov wrote about it all his life.

This is the only time we see them together: without any of the others; against all the others. All the rest are just intruders into this close circle. Think of it they are all almost the same age, maybe Anna is a bit older, maybe not. I couldn't find anything about her age in the play.

Actor: She's twenty seven.

Dodin: It doesn't say. It's not stated anywhere.

Actor: By some indirect quotes it can be calculated that she's under thirty.

Actor: Twenty eight – twenty nine.

Dodin: But there aren't any direct indications of Anna's age. They always play her as a mature woman. (Assumes Platonov's role): "So

this is friendship, is it? I've never been much good at it. I've always been better at love. A toast, come on, a toast. May this friendship end as it began." It's a very interesting statement, this explanation of friendship.

Actor: There is this premonition that...

Dodin: That everything is falling apart...

Actor: Falling apart, and very fast.

Dodin: (Improvises as Platonov addressing Anna): "I have this gut feeling that I'm losing you. I'm overwhelmed by all sorts of emotions too. How much I wish I were allowed just to love! And how much I hate you! Not least because of all this that we've just realised. Why can't we perish with dignity? Why always wriggle and quibble our way out, and cling to some meagre hope, just to hold on? How I wish that everything was different!... At a moment like this one can really feel like shouting or singing or stamping one's feet. It is definitely that kind of moment. (Sings) 'Find me a harness for my three fine horses...'"

Shall we continue or would you'd rather get your breath back? We'd better... So many things flash through one's mind... We should have gone somewhere, to a village to practise our steps... We didn't think of it...

The Play With No Name (*Platonov*), MDT, 1997.
The last rehearsal before the opening night.
Photographer Victor Vasilyev

Alexander Zavyalov
as Bugrov
Arkadiy Koval
as Porfiri Glagolyev
Sergey Kuryishev
as Platonov
Igor Nikolaev as Osip

BIBLIOGRAPHY
The following publications were used as sources for this book:

Dodin, L. 'Zametki na kazhdyi den', ('Notes for Every Day'), *Theatre*, no. 5 (1983)

Dodin, L. 'Strast k pravde', ('Passion for the Thruth'), *Izvestia*, 18 January, 1986

Dodin, L. 'Zachem rezhiseru kompania', ('Why Does a Director Need His Own Company'), *Teatralnaia Zhizn*, no.18 (1986)

Levikova, E. 'Chetyre dialoga i monolog na temy St. Peterburgskikh "Besov"', ('Four Dialogs and a Monologue on the themes of St. Petersburg's "Demons"'), *Sovremennaia Dramaturgia*, no. 5-6 (1992)

Dodin, L. 'Chernaya rabota po preodoleniiu samikh sebia', ('The Tough Job of Getting the Better of Oneself'), *Moskovskii Nabliudatel*, no. 7/8 (1992)

Dodin, L. 'Chudo po raspisaniu', ('Miracles Created to Order'), *Moskovskie Novosti*, 2 May (1993)

Dodin, L. 'Tolko na repetitsii mozhno zhit', ('You Can Only Live at Reherearsal!'), *Nevskoe Vremia*, 14 May (1994)

Dodin, L. 'Beg za zhizniu, kotoraia bystree tvoego shaga', ('Chacing Life That Is Faster Than You'), *Sovetskaia Kultura*, 14 May (1994)

Dodin, L. 'Ia ne khochu kazatsia optimistom, potomuchto takovym ne iavliaius', ('I Don't Want to Look Like an Optimist Because I Am Not'), *Art-fonar*, no. 5 (1994)

Dodin, L. 'Prostye Istiny', ('Simple Truths'), *Rossiiskaia Provintsia*, no. 2 (1995)

Dodin, L. 'Cheloveku s chelovekom trudno, emu I s soboi ne legko', ('It's Tough to Live with Others, It's Not Easy with Oneself Either'), *Argumenti i fakti*, no. 43 (1995)

Dodin, L. 'Klaustrofobia – izvechnaia bolezn cheloveka', ('Claustrophobia – the Everlasting Illness of Man'), *Moskovskie novosti*, 12–19 November (1995)

Dodin, L. 'Chelovek sushchestvo tragicheskoe, I emu neobkhodimo tragicheskoe iskusstvo', ('Man is a Tragic Being and He Needs a Tragic art'), Izvestia, 6 May (1997)

Dodin, L. 'Razmyshleniia v doroge', ('Thoughts on the Road'), *Nesavisimaia gazeta*, 8 August (1997)

Dodin, L. 'Chetyre monologa', ('Four Monologues'), *Obshaia gaseta*, 7-13 August (1997)

Dodin, L. 'Tolko s godami ponimaesh naskolko eto mojet byt khorosho – teatr!', ('Only With Age You Understand Just How Good Theatre Can Be!'), *St.Petersburg University*, 22 January (1998)

Dodin, L. 'Ia ne liubliu to, chto suzhaet mysl', ('I Don't Like the Things That Narrow Your Mind'), *Smena*, 15 April (1998)

Dodin, L. 'Nado byt v Rosii dolgozhitelem, daby chto-to o nei poniat', ('You Have to be Octogenarian in Russia in Order to Understand Anything about It'), *Nevskoe Vremia*, 2 October (1998)

Dodin, L. 'Idushchie po kanatu', ('Walking the Tight Rope'), *Rozhdestvenskie vstrechi*, Novosibirsk (1999)

Dodin, L. 'Zritel nikogda ne znaet, chto on khochet uvidet', ('The Spectators Never Know What They Want to See'), *Petrovskii kurier*, 6 September (1999)

Dodin, L. 'Interviu', ('Interview'), *Puls*, October (1999)

Dodin, L. 'Metafizicheskaia "Pikovaia dama"', ('The Metaphysical *Queen of Spades*'), *Russkaia mysl*, 21 – 27 October1 (1999)

Dodin, L. 'Nastoiashchii teatr – eto vsegda pro menia', ('Theatre – It's Always about Myself'), *Ekran i Stsena*, no. 13 (2000)

Dodin, L. 'Eto pochti fiziologicheskaya potrebnost – tvorit', ('It Is an Almost Physiological Need – to Create'), *AiF-Peterburg*, no. 48 (1998)

Dodin, L. 'Nedochitanye prorochestva', ('Unfinished Prophecies'), *Sezony*, no. 1 (1999)

Ivanova, L. 'Dodinu nravitsia chto zhizn eto p'esa bez nazvaniia', ('Dodin Likes It That Life Is a Play With No Name'), *Argumenti i fakti*, no. 43 (1997)

Kasumova, A. Interview with Lev Dodin for *Radio Russia*, 16 October 2000

Kovalenko, U. 'Lev Dodin: Chem trudnee zhizn tem produktivnee iskusstvo', ('The More Difficult Is Life, the More Productive Is Art'), *Izvestia*, 3 February (1994)

Nacharova, I. 'Sezon otkryli "Besy"', ('The Season Opened with "The Possessed"'), *Izvestia*, 20 October (1998)

Siminov, Vl. 'Daite slovo mame Dodina', ('Give the Floor to Dodin's Mother'), *Londonskii kurier*, no.7 (1997)

The translation of *Platonov* used in the book is from: Chekhov, A. *PLATONOV*, Adapted by **David Hare**, *Faber and Faber*, 2001

The translation of *Uncle Vanya* used in the book is from: Chekhov, A. *Plays*, Translated by **Michael Frayn**, *Methuen*, 1993

CHRONOLOGY OF PRODUCTIONS

1. *Invitation After the Execution...* by V. Dolgy. Staged by Zinovy Korogodsky, directed by Lev Dodin. Set Designer G. Berman. Leningrad Young Viewers' Theatre (LYVT), 1967

2. *Our Circus.* Staged and written by Zinovy Korogodsky, Lev Dodin and F. Filshtinsky. Set Designer Z. Arshakuni. LYVT, 1968

3. *The Master,* based on Gorky's *The Master* and *Konovalov.* Staged by Zinovy Korogodsky, directed by Lev Dodin. Set Designer Alexey Poray-Koshits. LYVT, 1968

4. *Model 18-68* by B. Goller. Staged by Zinovy Korogodsky, directed by Lev Dodin. Set Designer N. Ivanova. LYVT, 1968

5. *Ours and Only Ours...* Staged and written by Zinovy Korogodsky, Lev Dodin and F. Filshtinsky. Set Designer Marina Azizyan. LYVT, 1969

6. *Fairytales by Chukovsky.* Staged and written by Zinovy Korogodsky, Lev Dodin and F. Filshtinsky. Set Designers Z. Arshakuni, N. Polyakova, Alexey Poray-Koshits, V. Solovieva. LYVT, 1970

7. *The Lost Squadron* by A. Korneychuk. Staged by Zinovy Korogodsky, directed by Lev Dodin. Set Designer V. Dorrer. LYVT, 1970

8. *The Open Lesson.* Staged and written by Zinovy Korogodsky, Lev Dodin and F. Filshtinsky. Set Designer Alexey Poray-Koshits. LYVT, 1971

9. *What Would You Choose?* by A. Kurgatnikov. Set Designer M. Smirnov. LYVT, 1971

10. *Mess-Mend* by V. Menshov based on the novel by M. Shaginyan. Staged by Zinovy Korogodsky, directed by Lev Dodin. Set Designer M. Kitaev. LYVT, 1973

11. *It's a Family Affair—We'll Settle It Ourselves* by Alexander Ostrovsky. Set Designer Eduard Kochergin. LYVT, 1973

12. *The Robber* by Karel Capek. Design by Eduard Kochergin, costumes by Inna Gabay. Maly Drama Theatre (MDT), 1974

13. *Rosa Berndt* by G. Hauptman. Set Designer L. Mikhaylov. Leningrad Theatre of Drama and Comedy, 1975

14. *The Minor* by Denis Fonvizin. Design by Eduard Kochergin, costumes by Inna Gabay. Leningrad Theatre of Drama and Comedy, 1977

15. *The Rose Tattoo* by Tennessee Williams. Design by M. Kitaev, costumes by Inna Gabay. MDT, 1977

16. *The Appointment* by A. Volodin. Set Designer M. Kitaev. MDT, 1978

17. *Brothers and Sisters* based on Abramov's trilogy *Pryasliny.* Staged by A. Katsman and Lev Dodin. Set Designer N. Bilibina. Student Theatre at the Leningrad State Theatre, Music and Cinema Institute, 1978

18. *Live and Remember* based on Valentin Rasputin's novel. Design by Eduard Kochergin, costumes by Inna Gabay. MDT, 1979

19. *Love's Labours Lost* by William Shakespeare. Staged by A. Katsman and Lev Dodin. Set Designer N. Bilibina. Student Theatre at the Leningrad State Theatre, Music and Cinema Institute, 1979

20. *If Only, If Only...* staged by A. Katsman and Lev Dodin. Student Theatre at the Leningrad State Theatre, Music and Cinema Institute, 1979

21. *Don Juan Continued* by Eduard Radzinsky. Design by M. Kitaev, costumes by Olga Savarenskaya. Leningrad Comedy Theatre, 1980

22. *The House* based on Abramov's novel. Design by Eduard Kochergin, costumes by Inna Gabay. MDT, 1980

23. *A Gentle Creature* based on Dostoevsky's short story. Design by Eduard Kochergin, costumes by Inna Gabay. Leningrad Bolshoy Drama Theatre, 1981

24. *The Brothers Karamazov* based on Dostoevsky's novel. Staged by A. Katsman, Lev Dodin and A. Andreev. Set Designer N. Bilibina. Student Theatre at the Leningrad State Theatre, Music and Cinema Institute, 1983

25. *Oh, Those Stars!* staged by A. Katsman, Lev Dodin and A. Andreev. Student Theatre at the Leningrad State Theatre, Music and Cinema Institute, 1983

26. *The Golovlev Family* based on Saltikov-Shchedrin's novel. Design by Eduard Kochergin, costumes by Inna Gabay. Moscow Art Theatre, 1984

27. *The Bench* by A. Gelman. Staged by Lev Dodin, directed by E. Arie. Set Designer D. Krymov. MDT, 1984

28. *A Gentle Creature* based on Dostoevsky's short story. Design by Eduard Kochergin, costumes by Inna Gabay. MKhAT, 1985

29. *Brothers and Sisters* based on Abramov's trilogy *Pryasliny*. Design by Eduard Kochergin, costumes by Inna Gabay. MDT, 1985

30. *Lord of the Flies* based on William Golding's novel. Set Designer David Borovsky. MDT, 1986

31. *The Bankrupt* (*It's a Family Affair—We'll Settle It Ourselves*) by Alexander Ostrovsky. Design by Eduard Kochergin, costumes by Inna Gabay. Finnish National Theatre, Helsinki, 1986

32. *To the Sun* based on A. Volodin's one act plays. Set Designer M. Kitaev. MDT, 1987

33. *Stars in the Morning Sky* by A. Galin. Artistic director Lev Dodin, directed by T. Shestakova. Set Designer Alexey Poray-Koshits. MDT, 1988

34. *The Old Man* based on Yury Trifonov's novel. Design by Eduard Kochergin, costumes by Inna Gabay. MDT, 1988

35. *Returned Pages*, a literary reading. Staged by Lev Dodin, directed by V. Galendeev. Set Designer Alexey Poray-Koshits. MDT, 1988

36. *Gaudeamus* based on Sergey Kaledin's *Stroybat*. Set Designer Alexey Poray-Koshits. MDT, 1990

37. *The Possessed* based on Dostoevsky's novel. Design by Eduard Kochergin, costumes by Inna Gabay. MDT, 1991

38. *The Broken Pitcher* by Heinrich von Kleist. Artistic director Lev Dodin, directed by V. Filshtinsky. Design by Alexander Orlov, costumes by Olga Savarenskaya. MDT, 1992

39. *Desire Under the Elms* by Eugene O'Neill. Design by Eduard Kochergin, costumes by Inna Gabay. MDT, 1994

40. *The Cherry Orchard* by Anton Chekhov. Design by Eduard Kochergin, costumes by Inna Gabay. MDT, 1994

41. *Claustrophobia* based on contemporary Russian prose. Set Designer Alexey Poray-Koshits. MDT, 1994

42. *Elektra* by Richard Strauss. Conducted by Claudio Abbado. Set Designer David Borovsky. Salzburg Easter Festival, 1995

43. *Elektra* by Richard Strauss. Conducted by Claudio Abbado. Set Designer David Borovsky. Teatro Communale. Maggio Musicale Fiorentino 1996

44. *The Play With No Name* (*Platonov*) by Anton Chekhov. Design by Alexey Poray-Koshits, costumes by Irina Tsvetkova. MDT, 1997

45. *Lady Macbeth of the Mtsensk District* by Dmitry Shostakovich. Conducted by S. Bychkov. Set Designer David Borovsky. Teatro Communale. Maggio Musicale Fiorentino, 1998

46. *The Queen of Spades* by Piotr Tchaikovsky. Conducted by S. Bychkov. Set Designer David Borovsky. Netherlands Opera, Amsterdam, 1998

47. *The Queen of Spades* by Piotr Tchaikovsky. Conducted by V. Yurovsky. Set Designer David Borovsky. Opera National de Paris, 1999

48. *Mazepa* by Piotr Tchaikovsky. Conducted by M.Rostropovitch. Set Designer David Borovsky. La Scala, 1999

49. *Chevengur* by Andrey Platonov. Design by Alexey Poray-Koshits, costumes by Irina Tsvetkova. MDT, 1999

50. *Molly Sweeney* by Brian Friel. Design by David Borovsky, costumes by Irina Tsvetkova. MDT, 2000

51. *The Seagull* by Anton Chekhov. Design by Alexey Poray-Koshits, costumes by Khloya Obolenskaya. MDT, 2001

52. *The Moscow Choir* by Ludmila Petrushevskaya. Staged by Lev Dodin, directed by Igor Konyaev. Design by Alexey Poray-Koshits. MDT, 2002

53. *The Demon* by Anton Rubinstein. Conducted by Valery Gergiev. Set Designer David Borovsky. Costumes by Khloya Obolenskaya. Paris, Theatre du Chatelet (Theatre musical de Paris), 2003

54. *Uncle Vanya* by Anton Chekhov. Set Designer David Borovsky. MDT, 2003

55. *Otello* by Giuseppe Verdi. Conducted by Zubin Mehta. Set Designer David Borovsky. Florence, Teatro Comunale, 2003

56. *Salome* by Richard Strauss. Conducted by James Conlon. Set Designer and costumes David Borovsky. Paris, Opera-Bastille, 2003.

ILLUSTRATIONS

INDEX